Animal Tales
of the West

Also by the author:
Never Again, Vols. 1, 2, and 3

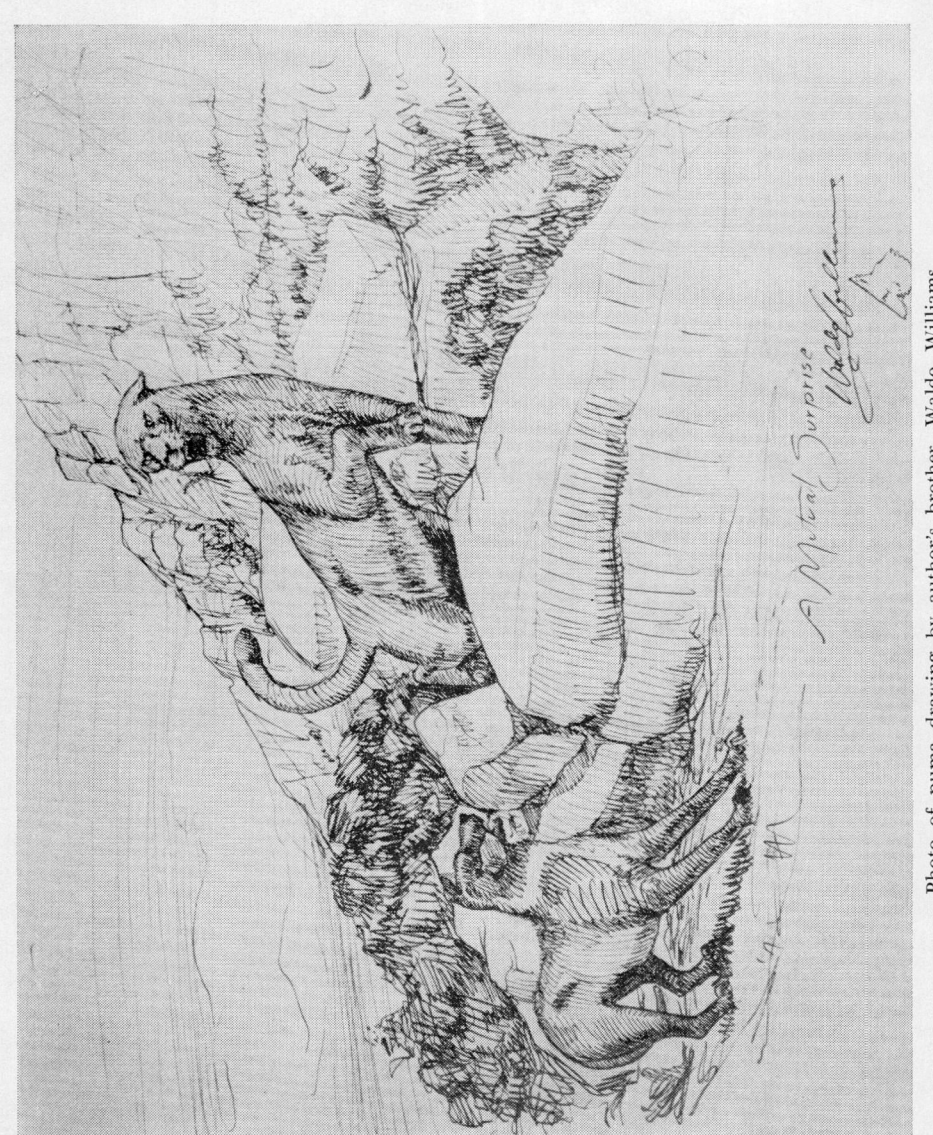

Photo of puma drawing by author's brother, Waldo Williams

Photo of mustang drawing by author's brother, Waldo Williams

Animal Tales of the West

by Clayton Williams

Illustrations by Bill Bristow

The Naylor Company
Book Publishers of the Southwest
San Antonio, Texas

Library of Congress Cataloging in Publication Data

Williams, Clayton, comp.
    Animal tales of the West.

    1. Animals, Legends and stories of. 2. Zoology--
The West. I. Title.
QL791.W536   599'.0978   74-22404
ISBN 0-8111-0538-5

Imperial Public Library
Imperial, Texas

2725

Copyright © 1974 by THE NAYLOR COMPANY

This book or parts thereof may not be reproduced without written permission of the publisher except for customary privileges extended to the press and other reviewing agencies.

ALL RIGHTS RESERVED

Printed in the United States of America

Contents

Introduction	vii
The Buffalo (American Bison)	1
The Mustangs	13
The Puma (A Large Wild Animal of the Cat Family)	29
The Bear (Black) — The Genus Euarctos Americanus	57
The Coyote (Canis Latrans)	69
The Lobo (A Large Member of the Canine or Wolf Family)	96
The Lynx and the Wildcat or Bobcat	112
The Ring-Tailed Cat and the Raccoon (Bassariscus and Procyon lotor)	126
The Fox (Vulpes macrotis)	139
The American Badger (Taxidea Taxus)	148
The Skunk	158
The Jackrabbit and Cottontail	180
The Peccary (Tayassuidae)	195
Cimarrons or Big Horn Sheep (Bovidae, bovinae, antilopinae)	205
The Prairie Dog (Cyonomys ludovicianus)	210

Introduction

Many pages in the following chapters consist of articles written by O. W. Williams in 1908 for the first publications of the Fort Stockton, Texas, *Pioneer*, a weekly newspaper. Later, this material was published in a brochure under the title, "Historic Review of Animal Life in Pecos County." I think it is important enough to justify publication of a great portion of it in book form.

O. W. Williams, a Harvard law graduate, came from Illinois to the rough Texas frontier in 1877. He was a pioneer surveyor in the Panhandle of Texas until 1879, prospected and rode horseback over much of New Mexico until 1882, and then evaluated timber land in East Texas until 1884. He then journeyed to Fort Stockton as a deputy county surveyor and did considerable surveying in Pecos County.

Another book written by Williams, *Pioneer Surveyor — Frontier Lawyer*, contains many of his experiences. At the time he came to Pecos County, the Indians had ceased to be a menace and the stockmen were moving in. Williams also served for a number of years as county judge of Pecos County. During the years from 1889 to 1901, he owned and operated a large farm and small ranch on the Pecos River. From his experiences in surveying, ranching, farming and research, he wrote some of his episodes and communicated his valuable observations of the animal life in this region.

In reading the Judge's "Historic Review of Animal Life in Pecos County," Gaines Kincaid, formerly of Fort Stockton and now of Austin, states:

> In so many of his writings, he was always such an ecologist and a "preserve the endangered species" proponent, many years before the idea got popular and essential. But with Señor Lobo, it was a different matter. Here, as never before, he is practically saying, "Kill the son-of-a-bitch!"

Besides Judge Williams' writings, I have made use of additional stories about West Texas animals, including taped interviews with professional trappers and others who have hunted and studied predators in this area during the present century. You will read of Tom Moore and Ernest Riggs, who loved the chase; Lloyd and Ed Ligon, pioneer ranchmen; and the escapades of the late, unforgettable Monte Wallace and Charlie Stone, old, experienced trappers who forgot more than many of us ever knew about wildlife. Also included are the stories of three of the Judge's children.

In 1891, Pecos County Commissioner's Court paid for the scalps of 764 coyotes at two dollars each; 31 wildcats at one dollar each; 8 panthers at five dollars each; 2 lobos at five dollars each; and 976 jackrabbits at one dollar per dozen. During the following year it paid for 1,042 coyotes, 65 wildcats, 2,204 rabbits, 9 panthers and 3 lobos along with a few prairie dogs.

At that time Judge Williams' family lived on his ranch and farm on the Pecos River. About 1930, a number of Texas counties, including Pecos, became a part of a state program which was a joint effort to control predatory animals. The information in the book covers much of the subsequent period, and was given to me by Charlie Stone, who has been employed for the last forty years as a predatory animal trapper.

With consumers paying such high prices for meat and

wool, it is imperative that the shackles placed on the livestock producer by Congress, under pressure of certain ecological groups, be removed. In view of the rapid increase of our human population, protein and wool should be preserved for the consumption of people, and not for predatory wild animals.

I understand that the use of poison, cyanide guns, and varmint drives using airplanes or helicopters have either been banned or can only be used by special bureaucratic permission. The end result of this is that the coyote is especially on the increase in this country.

This same kind of political pressure delayed, by several years, the construction of the oil pipeline from the great oil field in Alaska to the United States at a time when we are dangerously short on energy.

Members of the West Texas Chamber of Commerce are presently requested to contact their congressmen and urge them to make changes in the current ban on the use of chemical toxicants for predator control. Livestock producers say there is growing concern over the increase in loss of livestock to predators. It is said that these losses have increased so drastically, they threaten to put some producers out of business.

The following was stated in a recent meeting of the Texas Sheep and Goat Raiser's Association:

> In a recent survey a total of 35,940 producers were contacted, and of this number 15,685 producers responded. Six thousand of these producers were experiencing a loss from predators. Over 66,778 sheep and goats and over 6,179 calves were reported lost just to coyotes. Other predators were blamed for the death of 44,111 sheep, goats and cattle. Not only was this a loss to the producer but to the consumer's market, which might have had 10,000,000 more pounds of red meat available.

According to reports, in Pecos County, Texas, ranchers Burch and Louis Woodward and Roy Neal McKenzie have gone out of the sheep business. C. R. McKenzie has only one thousand more sheep for sale, and then plans to go out of the business.

Ten years ago there were 100,000 breeding ewes in Culberson County. Now there are none — largely due to the inroads by predators. The producers cannot offset this loss when they have been forbidden the use of all known devices to get rid of predators.

The Buffalo
(American Bison)

Some 15,000 years ago the vegetation growing on the lower Pecos was very similar to what we have today. The elephant, camel, horse and a very large species of bison roamed the region. The remains of a now extinct species of bison were dated back to about 8,200 B.C. It appeared that they had been driven over the canyon rim in order to butcher them in the rock shelter. Another deposit of burned, cut, and broken bones of bison was dated about 900 B.C.

Judge Williams was quite familiar with the plains buffalo. During one survey, he faced a stampeding herd and fired his gun again and again. As a result of his quick action, the rampaging and frightened animals divided in front of his survey crew, team and wagon and no one was trampled. Let us turn to his writings for a bit of history on the buffalo.

> According to zoologists, we should call this animal a bison; but I shall use the term by which it was known to the frontier settlers, who knew it best. Europeans found it to be the largest and most important indigenous animal on the North American continent. Fossil remains indicate that it has been here a long time, possibly longer than the Indians. At various times it has inhabited every area in the country, with the possible exception of the strip between Hudson Bay and the Gulf of St. Lawrence. In the sixteenth century it was not found in the Tidewater region of Virginia, nor along the Atlantic coast in New England, nor in Florida, Louisiana, and west of the Rocky Mountains.
> Yet it was found in New York, and Massachusetts settlers first heard of it around Lake Champlain. Later the town of Buffalo derived its name due to the presence of buffalo in very early times. It was present in Virginia, just back of the Blue Ridge. According to Abbe Jontel, LaSalle's French colony on Lavaca Bay in Texas used it for daily bread during the seventeenth century. In 1520, when Cortez entered the City of Mexico, the ruler, Montezuma, had a remarkable collection of birds, beasts and reptiles in his gardens. There was a buffalo in his menagerie. It was not found in the empire of Montezuma, which extended about as far north as the present Mexican state of Durango. It was probably brought to Mexico by one of a powerful clan of merchants and traders who located their headquarters in Mexico City. In about 1535, when Cabeza de Vaca journeyed across the southern part of Texas, he records that he ate the meat of this animal only three times. This must have been during his captivity around Lavaca Bay, where LaSalle's starving colonists used it for sustenance about 100 years later.

This would seem to indicate that the buffalo increased during those years, or some cause was set in motion to extend its range.

When de Vaca returned to Mexico from his wandering in Texas, Chihuahua and Sonora, he told a story of the Kingdom of Cibolo. According to him, great, rich and populous towns lay to the north of his route. Cibolo was an Indian name for the buffalo. In 1540, Coronado took quite an army of soldiers and made an extensive trip, searching for this kingdom of the Cibolo. He determined that if such a kingdom existed, it was confined to the community houses of the Zunis and Pueblo Indians of Northwestern New Mexico. Although there were plenty of buffalo robes in those towns, the animal itself was not found. He found countless numbers of buffalo on the plains, after going northeast from the head of the Pecos River. This locality seems to have been the favorite home of the animal, and it was here that it last appeared in the wild.

As early as the sixteenth century, the buffalo was sighted east of the Pecos. Juan de Oñate sent Sgt. Maj. Vincente de Zaldivar Mendoza and sixty mounted soldiers from the region in present-day New Mexico to the east side of the Pecos River to procure meat. The inexperienced soldiers attempted to drive the buffalo into corrals they had built. The unmanageable animals stampeded, killed a number of horses and injured forty soldiers.

In 1684, Juan Dominguez de Mendoza, a group of priests, soldiers and Jumanos Indians moved east from the present site of Fort Stockton to the Pecos River. They crossed the river, discovered a salt lake, and killed six buffalo.

Judge Williams gives us further information on the buffalo's choice of homes:

> It has been frequently stressed that the buffalo was never found west of the Pecos River. For several rea-

sons this appears true, if used in the sense that its regular habitat or home was never located west of that river. Beyond question, it was not found west of the Rocky Mountains. It WAS found IN the Rocky Mountains. It was often found among the valleys of those mountains opening to the east, where access was easy. An English traveler, Ruxton, found an abundance of buffalo in the South Park in Colorado around 1846. Lewis and Clark found it in the northern valleys of the Rocky Mountains at a much earlier date. Today, a remnant of free buffaloes are kept by the government in Yellowstone Park. I can find only one instance mentioning the presence of buffalo west of the Continental Divide.

Fifty years ago, [in 1858] the three most characteristic animals of the great plains were the buffalo, the antelope and the coyote. Though they existed in maximum numbers in that part of the country, none of these animals was exclusively a plains animal. When we first begin to find accounts of our country, some 300 years ago, many sections appear to be barren of buffalo. Yet, at that time, the buffalo was as much at home in the woods as he was on the plains.

In Arkansas, in the seventeenth century, LaSalle's party found it near the mouth of the Arkansas River. In the same century, English settlers found it along the Appalachians from North Georgia to Lake Ontario. Until the latter part of the eighteenth century, it was a common inhabitant in the forests in Ohio and Kentucky. The first English settlement of Western Tennessee was established at the old French Lick of Charville, now Nashville. During the first difficult winter, these settlers sustained life by the fruits of the hunt and the chase. They stocked their larders with buffalo meat. In the fall of 1781, one hunting party returned from a trip up a branch of the Cumberland River with the carcasses of 90 deer, 250 bears, and 75 buffaloes.

But fifty years ago man wielded his hoe, his axe, and his plowshare and contested the beast for dominion of the forest. Man wrested away the primeval home of the beasts and emerged the victor. Consequently, it is not surprising that the people of that day considered the buffalo strictly a plains animal. When millions of buffalo migrated over the plains, people were convinced that it was the dominant animal in those treeless wastes.

The coyote was present in the forests and parks farther east, but it was never a prominent animal in the world of the glades. Eventually it lost its small foothold east of the Mississippi. However, it remained one of the lords of the plains and in the wake of legions of buffalo, great numbers of coyotes toiled at the harvest.

The antelope, never a denizen of the woods in historic times, was one of the three animals most distinctively a product of the plains. It also inhabited the parks and inter-mural plains of the Rocky Mountains. It was not as numerous and significant as the buffalo, and along with the coyote it was classified as a second rate animal on the great plains.

Regular migrations of the buffalo indicate that it seldom traveled from east to west. Otherwise, it would have eventually crossed the Great Divide and become settled in favorite haunts west of the Rocky Mountains. It appears that impelling instinct drove them to wander from north to south, parallel to the chain of the Rockies, which served as a barrier to the west.

Roughly, the Rio Grande may be considered the southern limit of these migrations, although, in his monograph on the buffalo, Hornaday places it about 300 miles south of Eagle Pass. One wonders if the tough skin and heavy coat of hair did not evolve as a protection against a cold, northern climate. The animal seems best suited to this type of environment. However, as it multiplied, the buffalo was compelled to extend its range in order to forage for food, hence its migratory habits probably arose from necessity. If the animal's original home was in the plains east of the Rocky Mountains, then its extension to the south and east was a natural development. Along the northern and southern migrations lay the great plains best suited to it. The length of its migrations probably depended on its increase or decrease. If at any time it made its home to any extent in Pecos County, it was during a particularly prolific era among buffalo herds.

If the buffalo penetrated the Rocky Mountains further north, then farther south it might as easily have crossed the Pecos River. The Rockies lay west of the Pecos and are much more open at this location, without the same rock barrier in the latitude of 32 degrees that they have from the parallel of 37 degrees to the north. This is true — but then another consideration enters the field.

The buffalo requires an abundance of water. Once a day it must have plenty of water. When thirsty, I have seen them plunge into water and stand there drinking, oblivious of men on horseback racing among them, shooting them down. In the northern plains and parks of the Rocky Mountains melting snow generally furnished an abundance of water to the streams during the dry season. In its north and south migration, the buffalo drank at these streams which ran east and west and were fairly close together.

As we journey further south, this condition changes drastically. Close to the 37th parallel of latitude, a vast, high, dry plateau, known as the Llano Estacado butts out from the Rocky Mountains to the east. The eastern and northeastern rim of this plateau is largely a precipitous rocky front from 100 to 400 feet high. There are long stretches where a goat could hardly climb. In its northeastern circuit, there are few places where a buffalo could easily ascend. Once the top of this plateau has been gained, the surface is almost barren of water, and there is absolutely no shade. Pursued by buffalo hunters, desperation forced the animal to this plateau to make its last stand, but this location was never frequented by the beasts, for the environment was totally unsuited to its needs. I first set foot on the Llano Estacado in 1877, and this fact became very evident to me. The ground was deeply scarred with many buffalo trails in the low country, but on the plateau I found only four or five trails near water. In a radius of 4,000 square miles, the diminishing buffalo herds were making their last stand.

At the plateau, the buffalo which were migrating south, veered to the east side far enough to travel along the north to south line where the head streams of the Red River, Brazos and Colorado carried sufficient water to supply its daily needs. The animal followed that line to the southern limit of its migration. At about the 33rd parallel of latitude the rim of the Llano Estacado sloped off to a level that presented no obstacle to its passage. But a severe drouth existed in this section and the buffalo avoided it. There was a vast expanse of land between the heads of the Colorado and the Pecos Rivers which was totally devoid of water, hence the buffalo would not turn west again into this area. I assume that this is the natural condition which must have influenced the buffalo to avoid the country through which the Pecos River flows.

Accordingly, accounts of early travelers rarely mention sighting the buffalo west of a line drawn 100 miles east of the Pecos River. There is scant information on this section prior to 1850, at which time conditions changed and more extensive travel through this area began. In subsequent years an abundance of records was gathered. None of them which I have read mention the buffalo west of the Pecos River.

Nevertheless, men who are still living have seen them in Pecos County. Juan Cano Sr. told me that during the 1860's he spotted a herd of 25 or 30 near Leoncito Spring in the west part of the county. Benito Flores says he saw three head near Horsehead Crossing about 1870. There is other evidence that they were once present in this area. Twenty years ago, S. A. Purinton found buffalo horns on his ranch. I have heard reports of several other parties who found horns in the county. I will also relate a curious story which was told to me by S. J. Hensley of Presidio County. It is rumor, and his sources were not absolutely reliable. It may or may not be true, but it serves to enlighten us on early conditions in this country.

In its early years, the Mexican government recruited its army from convicted criminals. When sentence was passed on a convicted thief or murderer, he might escape confinement by enlisting in the army for a fixed term. But this type of soldier could not be stationed in the towns and settlements, for he would surely desert. They adopted the plan of putting these criminals in regiments called "condemned regiments." These regiments were stationed among the Indians far out on the desolate, untamed frontier, where it was much safer for a soldier to remain with his regiment than to desert. One post used for this purpose was located about 20 miles northwest of Presidio del Norte. It was known as Vado de las Piedras [an old fortress located 25 miles northwest of Presidio del Norte on the Rio Grande]. In 1850, Gen. Emory referred to it politely as a place of "military colonists." At that time, he stated that it contained about 300 souls who were raising wheat and corn, irrigating these crops from a canal.

According to the story, they [the members of the condemned regiment] previously eked out a scanty living by hunting and farming. Buffalo meat was the most easily procured and preserved when they were available, so the colonists kept a sharp eye out for buffaloes. Sometime before 1850, in the fall of the year, they were informed that there was a herd of buffalo on the plains of San Estevan, 12 miles from Marfa. In recent years, San Estevan was noted throughout this country as a place where stone ollas [large-mouthed pots or jars] were manufactured out of a tufaceous stone found near the spring. When I last visited this place, Judge W. W. Bogel had established a ranch there.

Everything was immediately prepared for a great hunt. Guns were vetoed because powder was scarce. A body of mounted soldiers armed with lances and arrows was dispatched to San Estevan. They were accompanied by two-wheeled carretas pulled by oxen, and loaded with salt and equipment for jerking meat and preserving skins. When they arrived at their destination, the mounted men lost no time in attacking the herd. Everything was progressing smoothly. Buffaloes were being slain on every side, and glee was written on each face at the prospect of a bountiful harvest of meat. The men could almost taste a juicy buffalo steak cooked to perfection — when the proverbial apple cart (or buffalo cart in this instance) toppled over. Suddenly a band of Comanches swept upon the scene, spreading woe where joy had reigned. The Indians appropriated all the meat and a number of hunters' scalps for trophies. The frustrated Condemned Regiment raced back to the security of the military colony, where the survivors of the unfruitful buffalo hunt filled up on plain corn — "mais azul" — until the dreaded Comanches took their leave.

Whether or not this is true, the probability of such an occurrence was large in pioneer days. Certainly the military colony was there, and Comanches were customary marauders into Mexico during the frontier era. If true, it furnishes more evidence that small bands of buffaloes did occasionally go west of the Pecos.

One more scene: In the extreme southeast end of old Pecos County the San Francisco creek joins the Rio Grande River. It is a rugged and precipitous country. The creek and river have cut deep through a mesa of level limestone, and the bluffs that frown down over the river are probably 400 feet high, and so nearly perpendicular that there are only a few places where a man could descend to get a drink of water that can be seen in such abundance below. The relatively level surface between the creek and the river at the mouth of the creek forms a veritable cul de sac, or in our cowboy's expressive language, a "trap," into which cattle are always liable to drift and starve to death within sight and scent of the water for which they are famished.

When I first came to this country some 24 years ago, [1884] I heard a story concerning some Seminole scouts. They found a small herd of buffalo in this trap some years before, and when the animals saw that they were cornered by the Indians, they jumped off the bluff and were killed. It was said that there were many buffalo bones there, indicating that this had happened more than once, and that "trap" had been catching buffalo as it now catches cattle.

Although the buffalo is a magnificent animal, it had

only indirect influence on the history of Pecos County. The Indians could remain in this area only so long as the buffalo made its annual migration east of the Pecos River. To the primitive savage the meat meant sustenance, and the hide furnished clothing. Of course as long as the Indian remained, the cowman and settler would not come here. When the buffalo became extinct, desperation forced the Indian to the reservation. Then the cowman brought his herds westward. The influx of cattle in Pecos County dates from the extermination of the buffalo. Twenty years ago frontiersmen gave this answer to the sentimental tenderfoot when he bemoaned the murderous waste of the buffalo. Another bit of instructive information concerning the extinction of the buffalo is seldom alluded to these days. It may be well to mention it here:

The immediate cause for such wholesale destruction was a commercial reason. Buffalo hides brought from $3 to $5 each, and trained hunters could easily kill large numbers of the animals with the Sharps buffalo guns. Hunting them rapidly became an occupation which probably interested several thousand people. In those days the majority of the hunting was done in Kansas, Nebraska, Colorado and the Indian Territory, along and near the line of the Union Pacific and Kansas Pacific railroads.

About that time Congress passed a law forbidding the hunting of buffalo for the hides. Of course this law could only apply to the territories and was not effective in the states. To supplement it similar laws were passed by the states of Kansas, Nebraska and Colorado. This shut down hunters in those states. Texas failed to enact this law, hence Texas was the only place left to them. To make their work in that state count, buffalo hunters adopted this method:

As the buffalo moved south on their annual migration, the hunters trailed them. They established a cordon of hunters across the north end of the state, and when the buffaloes came back on the return migration, they were stopped and actually held in Texas by an army of men. They were never again allowed to cross that line into Kansas, but were held and finally exterminated in the Panhandle of Texas. In 1877, I saw them there by the thousands. In 1879, I saw but one small herd, as they had been practically annihilated. A few lingered on the plains for several years thereafter, and in 1885 John Valentine and I ate our last buffalo steaks at Cowden's Wells, twenty miles north of Monahans. Three remained with the TX cattle around Horsehead Crossing on the Pecos until about 1895. Their death spelled the last of the buffalo in this part of the country.

One of the early settlers of this region says he came across some Mexicans from the region of Presidio del Norte, Mexico, in 1877. They were salting butchered buffalo meat at the salt lake east of the Pecos River in present Crane County. Their kill had been made in that vicinity where the skins were first cut and then pulled off by horsepower.

Following the practice of the Cibolas Indians of Mexico, these Mexicans had followed the old Salt Trail from the region of Presidio del Norte. When they arrived at the salt lake mentioned above, they established what was afterward known as Salt Crossing in order to get their buffalo meat.

Like all other subjects, history has its lighter moments. The following tale was presented as truth:

During the 1870s two pioneers were hard up for food in the area between the high plains and the Pecos River. The hungry men spotted an old buffalo grazing in a large "hog-wallow" depression. To make sure they got their game, their strategy was to separate and advance on it from opposite directions. As one of them drew a bead on the animal, it charged the other one. Quite sensibly the latter avoided tangling with an enraged buffalo by promptly darting into a handy cave. The first hunter took careful aim once again. Before he could fire, the concealed partner leaped from the cave like a jack-in-the-box into what could have been the line of fire. This occurred several times before the buffalo was finally shot.

When the hunters reunited, the first one asked with exasperation, "John, why in the heck didn't you stay in that cave until I shot the buffalo?"

John replied, "I would have, but there was the goldern-dest bear in that cave you ever seed!"

The Mustangs

Fleet steed of the prairie, in vain men prepare
For thy neck arched in beauty, the treacherous snare;
Thou wilt toss thy proud head and with nostrils
    stretched wide
Defy them again as thou oft' has defied.

Ye may know him at once, though a herd be in sight,
As he moves o'er the plain like a creature of light,
His mane streaming forth from his beautiful form
Like a drift of a wave that has burst in the storm.

His fields have no fence save the mountain and sky;
His drink the snow-capped Cordilleras supply;

'Mid the grandeur of nature sole monarch is he,
His gallant heart swells with the pride of the free.

The state of animals in the new world, and wild mustangs in particular, were the subject in 1908 of this article by Judge Williams:

> The animals of the new world are not the same as those of the old world, but generally speaking, they are of the same families and are kin to each other. Now there are no large animals here, such as exist over the ocean. The elephant and camel are larger than any animal we have in America. If you take the different species of the same family, the new world species will not, as a rule, be found as large as the lion and tiger. . . . It was also claimed that the new world animals were not as highly specialized nor so well fitted for the struggle for survival as those of the old. This last contention is to some extent denied but the first is certainly true.
> From these premises were drawn the curious conclusion that the new world was not as efficient a mother to animal life and activity as the old: That a larger and higher grade of animal life was not possible here because nature could not support and maintain it: That the new continent had come out of the hands of the Creator prematurely, before it had ripened to a state capable of supporting a higher grade. This was seen even in the highest type of animal life — man himself. A handful of Europeans had conquered the Indians, and the Negro had been imported to take the place of Indian labor in mines and on plantations because the Indians had been found physically incompetent to the task, and were fast dying out under such hard labor.
> From this theory, it was thought to necessarily follow that the types of animals introduced from Europe would deteriorate and degenerate when introduced into this country. This was applied to man himself, and it was claimed by some writers that evidences of this degeneration were to be had in the history of

Europeans in the West Indies. Such a conclusion necessarily made some of us Americans a little warm. Solis, in his "History of Mexico," devotes one entire volume out of three to a refutation of this theory. Not more than twenty years ago a distinguished professor of Harvard College found it worth his while to write a book entitled *Man and Nature in America*, the object of which is to show that man has not physically or mentally deteriorated in America. As my ancestry goes back in America some 200 years, I have a special grievance against this theory, and I take pleasure in adding my mite to the defense by referring to the wild horse in our Southwest.

It is well known that the horse was introduced into America by the Spanish Conquistadores. It was a very material factor in their first conquest, because the natives believed it to be as much a supernatural being as the rider himself. When some intrepid Mexicans first succeeded in killing a horse they cut off its head and sent it to Montezuma, to prove to him that it was mortal. It was so necessary to the Spaniards that they introduced it as rapidly as possible, and it is probable that by 1540 the horse was running wild to some extent in Mexico. The Indians were quick to seize and utilize the horse once they understood its use and importance. Comanches and other tribes followed the migrating buffalo for food. They were often compelled to change camp with only the help of their large dogs who were taught to carry tepee poles. They naturally sought for such an animal as the horse. The system of barter among the Indians and the glory of horse-stealing contributed to a rapid spread of the horse over the Western and Southwestern plains of the United States and Mexico. Considering the primitive state of the Indians, it is probable they lost two horses to run wild where they were able to keep one.

In his narrative of the establishment of the Mission to the Tejas Indians, Don Damian Manzanet records that they encountered: "An Indian, a very tall youth on an excellent bay horse, hunting buffalo." This was "four days' journey" north of the San Marcos River in the year 1690. There are other notices of horses in Texas during the same period, so I think we can reasonably assume that we have had the wild horse here for at least 250 years. As I have stated above, if the horse was in the hands of the Indian, it must have been present in the feral [allowed to run wild or loose — herded] state. The Indians must have allowed many to escape, especially on their first acquaintance with the animal, when they were unfamiliar with its habits, and not prepared by any former experience to take care of it or recapture it.

Additional evidence of the many wild horses in Texas is furnished in a report given by A. Mezierres. Along with his two sons, Mezierres and a few soldiers took a course out of San Antonio in 1778 through the rough and trackless regions of southwest Texas, where the Comanches had previously had corrals and rancherías. There they found an incredible number of Castillian cattle and herds of mustangs around the Brazos and Colorado rivers. These herds were likely a portion of the 66,000 head of cattle and horses that had previously disappeared from the ranches of New Spain.

In 1801, Phillip Nolan, the horse trader, was catching wild horses near the site of Waco, Texas. A Spanish force attempted to arrest him. He resisted and was killed in the skirmish that followed. Evidently wild horses were attractive and profitable enough to invite the hazards encountered by their captors.

I now continue with Judge Williams' article:

> If there was any tendency to degeneration in this country in the horse, it must have appeared in 250 years of wild life. The horse, while under the direct care of man, might escape the result of such a tendency. It has escaped it, if such tendency exists, as it is a well known fact that America, today, produces some of the finest horses in the world. When England wanted horses for her army in the Boer War, she sent to the United States for the greater part of them rather than

buy them in Europe. This is excellent evidence for the quality of our horses, since an army horse is picked for its speed, stamina and endurance. Our polo players have money to throw to the winds and demand the best horses. They send to Texas for ponies and pay fancy prices for them, not only because of their training as cow ponies, but also due to their swiftness and endurance. Many of these army and polo horses have been bought in Pecos County.

Now let us turn to the wild horses that have been condemned to an existence upon this continent and left without the protecting care of man. How have they fared?

The wild horse has almost completely disappeared in Texas along with the buffalo. It, too, stood in the way of advancing civilization. The presence of these animals in a community was always a menace to horse owners and raisers, for it would toll off tame horses. Hence, ranchmen made war on it and exterminated it. But there are many men still living who have seen it wild and can testify to its excellence. Many stories are circulated of wild horses, aided by all the resources of man, yet the wild ones manifested speed and endurance equal to or greater than that of the tame horses.

I have not personally witnessed a practical test between tame and wild horses, but I know of nothing in the animal kingdom that can compare with the beauty and grace of the wild horse. More than 30 years ago our party was traveling slowly over the high plains in Floyd County, Texas. Early one morning we spotted a herd of wild horses galloping toward us more than two miles away. They had scented us and were coming to investigate. On the treeless plain we could see every sinuous curve on the proud, powerful animals. They came on in a straight line that deflected every now and then in a change of course denoting a pure wantonness of strength. As they drew closer, they formed a front with about 100 horses and bore down on us in a straight charge just as a company of cavalry might have done. At about 150 yards distance they suddenly stopped with that front one hundred deep. With heads held high, nostrils dilated, manes and tails sweeping the ground, they were magnificent objects of beauty.

Most of them were bays with a sprinkling of browns, duns and a few grays and cream colors. Their forms, as far as I could judge, presented models of equine beauty. I thought they were smaller than an average horse, but the symmetry of form and promise of speed lay in those slender limbs, rounded breasts and wide nostrils. After a few moments of inspection, they gave a snort of alarm and were off like a flock of birds to take flight in the same sinuous waving line of travel that characterized their approach.

I saw them many other times, sometimes only two or three in number, sometimes twenty or thirty, but rarely in greater numbers. I always remarked on the beauty of contour which they showed. I had seen a good many domesticated saddle horses which were supposed to have been captured from mustang herds, and none of them had this beauty of form, but were generally noted for angularity of form, and lack of rounded contour. I never understood this until I fell in with a Mexican and his captured herd of mustangs in Lubbock County, Texas, in the summer of 1878.

This man told me that he lived in Las Vegas, N. M., and came to these plains every year to capture wild horses. He carried them back to New Mexico, sold them and made a little money in the process. He was traveling with a wagon, two cows and calves. I do not know how he caught them, but he had about thirty colts — the most dejected, wretched looking specimens of horseflesh I think I ever saw. In order to control them he had tied each animal with a hair rope running from the tail to the fetlock joint of the foreleg. This rope had worn great raw bloody places on the inside of the thigh and around the fetlock. It was tied short, and the colts walked or trotted with a decided limp.

As a rule, all wild animals lose spirit and beauty when they are taken into captivity. It takes several generations born into captivity to bring about adaptation and acceptance of the new conditions. Until that time comes, the spirit of the animal appears to be under a cloud. Consider the natural results from good treatment — then consider the kind of barbarism to which the Mexican submitted these colts, and you cannot expect to have anything approaching the constitution and beauty of the wild animal. Every mustang captured in early days was subjected to similar treatment due to the fact that his captor was rarely able to keep him without brutal methods. Hence, almost invariably the degeneration in the animal's appearance manifested.

As to the stamina and appearance of the horse, I don't think that 250 years of wild life in Texas and Mexico has brought around any deterioration in him. Mother Nature in America has been as efficient a mother to the horse as she has in the wastes of North Africa, from where the ancestor of our wild horses probably came.

I have never understood why the wild horse was not found in greater abundance in Pecos County. It was found up and down the Pecos River, but nowhere else, and never in great numbers. The grass and water were here, and for the last 250 years the Indian occupation has not been sufficient to have disturbed it. The great Comanche War Trail leading to and from Mexico crossed through the middle of the county, and over this trail the Comanches drove thousands of stolen horses between 1820 and 1870. One would expect that the mere losses from the droves would have stocked the country with them.

I digress from the Judge's article to mention that some mustangs were left along the great Comanche War Trail in addition to those at Horsehead Crossing. Some forty-five miles east of Horsehead Crossing and on both the Comanche War Trail and the Butterfield mail route to Fort Stockton was Mustang Pond. The Ford Neighbor's party, in 1849 while scouting for a favorable route through the then unknown West Texas, came to this pond. They gave it the name because wild mustangs had caused their mules to break away in the early morning. It was noon before the animals were retrieved.

It is reasonable to speculate that there were very few mustangs west of the Pecos because the Apaches and other Indians ate them. There were very few or practically no buffalo west of the Pecos, according to all available records. Those mustangs or wild ones west of the Pecos, which had escaped from the Kiowas and Comanches en route back from Mexico, furnished more available meat for the Mescalero Apache. The Indian preferred the tender meat of the colt, so the offspring of the mustangs was the first to disappear.

Judge Williams' article continues:

> Yet when I came here some 24 years ago [1884] there was only one small herd ranging on the Pecos River near Horsehead Crossing. It was probably a herd that escaped from some Comanche raid. Sometime in the 1880s a man named Slaughter lost some stock horses near Horsehead Crossing, from a herd that he was moving to New Mexico or Arizona. These horses naturally fell in with the Mustangs. They were a nuisance to the country as every runaway horse wandered into this band and became an "outlaw."
>
> Mr. Herf Lyons, manager of the Baldridge Ranch about 25 miles northeast of Fort Stockton, says "there are only about 15 of this herd left." They are inferior animals and Lyons believes it is due to inbreeding and lack of new blood. It is evident that the career of the wild horse is about over in this country.

Because the Judge never finished his article on mustangs, I will continue the narrative.

A few years after Judge Williams wrote this article in 1908, the inferior herd of mustangs mentioned by Herf Lyons was run down. They were allowed to fill their stomachs in the Pecos and then were lassoed by a group of cowboys. The chief of that relay run was Richard Crosby, veteran stockman. He was the father of Bob Crosby, whose name was placed in the Cowboy Hall of Fame as the all-around champion cowboy of his time.

Professional mustangers used several methods to catch wild horses. In the brush country of southwest Texas, a circular pen, camouflaged within a thicket with wings leading to it, formed a trap into which the horses were driven. Sometimes snares were set on a trail leading to water to catch the mustang. Perhaps the cruelest way was to crease them, that is, shoot them so the bullet would just stun them by hitting below the mane and above the top of the neck bone, but not injure the spinal column. Reportedly, if the muscular part of the neck above the vertebrae was struck by the bullet, the horse would become paralyzed and fall to the ground. Before it could regain its senses the mustanger came up to it, sidelined, hobbled or clogged it and placed a rope around its neck. More often than not, the animal was killed because the shot was not sufficiently accurate.

Many times wild horses were simply chased until they were exhausted. This was accomplished by relays of well-mounted men, stationed at intervals on frequently traveled routes used by the mustangs in their flight. Another method of trailing was likely used by the mustanger whose "dejected, wretched-looking specimens of horseflesh" so appalled Judge Williams. Professional mustangers who used this process followed a particular mare and her colt day and night — never allowing the colt to nurse nor the mare to eat. These two methods were used on the wide open spaces of the plains where one could see for miles and water holes were scarce and far apart.

In southwest Texas where brush and small timber were available, mustangs were either sidelined with rope hobbles or burdened with wooden clogs. A wooden clog was shaped like a *Y*. The inside of this *Y* was fastened to the horse's foreleg above the hoof. It greatly restricted his movements and enabled the mustanger to control him. Quite often they were necked to an old gentle horse or burro. The tame animal gentled the mustang to some extent, while also teaching it to lead.

According to the late J. Frank Dobie, some mustang stallions put up a courageous fight to retain their freedom. A big sorrel horse, weighing 1,000 to 1,200 pounds roamed the plains in the 1870s. Two cowboys were pursuing the herd in which this proud piece of horseflesh ran. One horseman chased the band while the other waited on top of a creek bluff to toss the loop over the neck of the unsuspecting stallion. The stallion followed the band up the trail. As prearranged, the mustanger dropped his loop over the mustang's head. Abruptly, the angry stallion headed straight for the horseman, struck him with his forefeet and dug his teeth deep into the mustanger's thigh, peeling off a portion of pants, skin and flesh.

The mustang charged again as the horseman pulled his six-shooter and fired. The noise and flash of the gun panicked the animal and he whirled to flee and hit the end of the rope. This mighty tug jerked the mustanger's horse into the dirt. The frightened mustanger had barely untangled himself from his horse and saddle when the furious stallion laid his ears back, opened his mouth and charged again with death in his eye. Only a timely shot from the mustanger's comrade saved the horseman's life. The bullet broke the horse's shoulder and stopped him only a few feet short of his intended victim.

In the 1880s a beautiful speedster called the Great White Stallion, or the Ghost of the Llano Estacado, roamed the plains. This splendid stallion exhausted so many relays of grain-fed horses to retain his freedom that he was known as the Ghost Horse. He refused to be captured. In his last tragic race he was followed by the Trujillos and their vaqueros on well-fed racehorses. The Great White Stallion continued running for miles and miles after his mares fell out.

Rather than lose his freedom, that magnificent animal

leaped from a thirty-foot bluff into the unknown. He landed on the white surface of Yellow House Lake, which was underlaid with a black, bottomless alkali bog. When his pursuers arrived, the Great White Horse of the Llano Estacado had almost sunk. Only the head and neck of the stately animal were visible as he vainly attempted to free himself from the mud. With each effort he sunk deeper and deeper until the muck covered his nostrils. He coughed several times, shook his head, and the Ghost of the Llano Estacado eluded his pursuers forever.

A white pacing stallion kept his "manada" (group of mares) in the Nueces country. He was chased for years without success. Finally, his time had come. The stallion and his mares were seen watering and twelve well-mounted men gave chase in relays. The horse headed first toward San Antonio, but on the second day he raced back toward his favorite range. When the band crossed the Guadalupe, his mares lagged behind. By the third day only the stallion was running; the remainder of the exhausted herd had fallen by the wayside.

At this point, abandoned by his harem, the stallion either paced or single-footed toward the Rio Grande. Even the well-mounted relay gave up. The great pacing stallion never returned to the Nueces country.

He was spotted by a vaquero who had heard of him and knew the great pacer for what he was. After eluding the twelve men, the tired stallion entered a boxed-in water hole to quench his immense thirst. The vaquero, concealed behind a thicket, threw his loop and caught the stallion. The horse had traveled over a hundred miles, running hard, pacing or single-footing without food or water. Although his endurance was fading, he showed plenty of grit when he felt the rope upon his neck and gauged its strength. He wheeled with wide open mouth and charged his captor. Fortunately the vaquero put a healthy mesquite between himself and the animal, and managed to snub the mustang to a tree.

The vaquero staked his magnificent catch with three ropes to prevent him from choking himself, and tied a clog to one of his forefeet. He carried water and placed it within reach of the horse. The proud stallion wouldn't take a nibble of food, nor a sip of water. He acted the part of "give me liberty, or give me death" until he died.

The following boyhood experiences with mustangs were recorded by my older brother, the late Oscar Waldo Williams, II. At the time the incidents occurred, he was living on the Judge's farm and ranch on the Pecos River in the 1890s.

> There were mustangs in the country then. The name mustang was our effort to pronounce the Spanish word mesteño in English. This word, meaning "wild one," referred to the many wild horses which were bred from the horses lost by the Spaniards during exploration days. In my time, these horses were hardly pure descendants of the Barbs and Arabs of the early Spaniard. Many of our tame horses ran off to the wild herds. Some of the worst of the wild horses bore well-known brands. I recall one old gelding burro that ranged between Fort Stockton and the Pecos River near Horsehead Crossing road. He had a map of Mexico on him. Most of us youngsters tried to catch him and failed. He would let us come within a hundred yards of him, then he would dash away. No matter how well we were mounted, we could never get within roping distance of him.
>
> Some years before my time on the Pecos River, John Slaughter had driven herds of cattle and horses through our terrain on his way to Cochise County, Arizona, where he later became famous as the fighting sheriff of Cochise. In our area a fine race stallion had quit him for the wild herd. Every year or so a crew would come in from the Slaughter ranch in Cochise County, Arizona and camp at various points to the east of our place and make another effort to recapture the fine gray horse which had got away from them. Father said that they came back two years in succession try-

ing to catch the runaway. I know that they caught several of the mustangs, but the escaped race horse was never caught. I presume he died on the wild range or was killed by a younger horse when he grew old. One of the captured mustangs broke his neck rather than submit to being led behind a wagon. This happened about three-fourths of a mile southeast of our ranch house in Santa Rosa Draw.

Willie Harrell and I once rode across the Salt Lake [that small depression just south of the present Imperial Reservoir], followed a little dip to the east, and came upon the band of wild horses. A great gray horse trotted out toward us with a proud, exaggerated stride. When all of his band had passed him, he whirled and followed them. This was the Slaughter horse. Later, the ranchmen caught many of his colts, mostly gray, and they were superior horses to have come from a mustang herd.

That herd, or another herd of mustangs, carried away three of our mules not long after I saw the herd. We had considerable trouble getting them back. One mule died from the excessive running involved in its capture and another mule stayed with them for over a year. We ran the herd as far east as Horsehead Crossing. At the end of three days two mules were separated from the band at Monument Springs, where one of the mules died. Three days of riding in relays with little to eat in the shifts between rides was a hard task. I recall eating while standing for several days thereafter.

I may have seen an offspring of the Slaughter stallion perform as a racehorse both at Fort Stockton and in Grandfalls. Northeast of the abandoned fort's parade ground, cowboys would frequently run horse races. Prior to the race, a cast-iron washpot was dragged through the burro grass to form a smooth trail for each horse to run on. Bets were placed and races were run prior to the time when horse racing and betting were outlawed.

At one of the races I saw a large horse the cowboys

called Two-and-a-Half. Reportedly he was roped from one of the mustang herds near Horsehead Crossing. The Mexican cowboy who roped him sold the small colt for $2.50 and thus developed the name for the mustang. He grew into a large horse and an attempt was made to break him as a draft horse. Elmer Moore, then a young cowboy on the Baldridge Ranch, managed to harness the animal to the wagon — but when the team was started, the mustang, Two-and-a-Half, reared back and fell against the wagon, breaking his tailbone as he did so.

He was ridden some as cow horse and found to be swifter than all of the cow ponies on the ranch. Later he was brought to Fort Stockton to try his speed there. It was then that I saw the horse. As he walked, he gave the impression he had a broken hip. The tail was broken so that it pointed a little to one side. One might have gotten the idea that his hip was knocked down. At any rate, it did give me the idea that the horse was slightly crippled, although he was a big, fine animal.

About a year later I was to see him race in Grandfalls, during a celebration. As a small boy I had ridden my pony behind the stage hack from Fort Stockton to Grandfalls to see the baseball game. The game was delayed until a horse race could be completed. I was annoyed at this delay, but took some notice of what was going on around me. The Baldridge cowboys were there with Two-and-a-Half. Some men were actively urging the Stockton and Baldridge cowboys to bet on old Two-and-a-Half. These men were holding off with their horse and tantalizing the sponsors of the Pecos County mustang to bet everything they had — even spurs, ropes, or anything that would do to barter.

About twenty-eight years later, Van Carr, formerly of Grandfalls, told me the full story. The Grandfalls horse-racing fans knew that Two-and-a-Half had beaten every horse in this region. They pooled together with some Midland financiers and sent to Kentucky for the fastest racing horse they could afford. It arrived at Grandfalls for the race harnessed as a buggy horse. It was driven to the racetrack in front of the buggy. In that position the bets were placed with the expectation that the Stockton boys would be easily taken. However, dependable old Two-and-a-Half upset the horse-cart for the financiers. The product of the Slaughter racehorse and a mustang mare beat the fancy Kentucky racehorse. Most of the gambling proceeds jangled in the pockets of happy, local cowboys.

Two-and-a-Half was then purchased by a dirt contractor, taken to Juarez, Mexico, and sold, where he ran on those racetracks for a number of years.

My friend, Jeanne Simmons, contributed the following information:

> Two-and-a-Half and other outstanding mustangs brought honor and glory to their owners — as well as money. One cannot discount the importance of horses to the white settlers who first came to this country. But to the Indian, the horse was of paramount importance. From a plodding foot-traveler, the horse elevated the Indian to a mobile warrior. With the introduction of the horse and the gun, the Indian became a formidable foe to be reckoned with.
>
> Without grain, the Indian ponies grew into a distinct breed, different from their pure Barb and Arab descendants, with a personality all their own. An adult mustang stallion averaged 14 hands high and weighed around 700 pounds. All of them were not particularly beautiful, but mostly tough, wiry, and rugged, and could often outrace army horses.
>
> In 1867, one army officer wrote: "The Indian pony, without stopping, can cover a distance of from 60 to 80 miles between sunrise to sunset, while most of our horses are tired out at the end of 30 or 40 miles . . . which means they (the Indians) always get away from us."
>
> An Indian youth was taught to ride at the age of six or seven, and in time almost became a part of his horse. Many of them displayed more kindness toward their ponies than they did toward their wives. Some

of them broke their horses by taking them into the water. When the horse tried bucking, his head went under a few times until he quieted down. The Indian usually rode a tame horse out of the water. Some historians say the Indians — especially the Sioux and Comanche — belong in the top two or three categories of best horsemen in the world.

The Puma
A Large Wild Animal of the Cat Family

In pioneer days Pecos and Brewster counties were infested with pumas, or panthers, as they were sometimes called by the natives. To the Mexican or Spaniard this feline is known as the Leon. Leon Water Holes, west of Fort Stockton, were so named because of the presence of these big cats. They gathered there to drink. A small spring in the northern part of Brewster County is known as

Leoncita. I have no idea whether this refers to a baby puma, lynx or a diminutive Leon Water Hole.

In 1873, the following incident was recorded by Maj. Zenas R. Bliss, who was riding ahead of an army wagon train en route from Fort Stockton to Fort Concho:

> We encamped on the banks of the Pecos River, and there was no settlement nearer than Fort Stockton, which we had left three days before. We had a talk with the station-keeper [Pecos Station or Camp Melvin], and he told us that his dogs, of which he had about half a dozen, had followed a pack of coyotes, and had been gone several days. He said they had frequently done so before but had always returned in less time than they had been absent. They eventually returned on that occasion, but afterwards I was told that they followed a pack off and were never seen again. They probably went so far that they became exhausted and died on the prairies.
>
> I left the Pecos quite early the morning after our arrival. It was raw and cold, and the air was filled with mist that made the surface of the ground in the road wet. Lt. Tear and I were on horseback and ahead of the wagons and ambulances. It was a wet norther and very chilly, and as we rode along, I said to Mr. Tear, that it would be a pretty good time to take a nip if anyone had anything of the kind. To my surprise, he said he had a bottle of "Hezoal" in his saddle pockets and when we got down into the valley, we were then on a little hill, we would have a nip. At the bottom of the hill where we were out of sight of the ambulances and their occupants, we stopped, and he produced a bottle.
>
> As we were standing there I noticed that something had been dragged across the road, and I thought a blanket had been drawn across the road, and I said, "Hello, there is an Indian sign." Mr. Tear immediately went to the left of the road, but on examination of the trail a little more closely, I saw that it was going to the right and in a few yards I discovered the large tracks of a mountain lion on each side of the thing

that was being carried off. A soldier just then made his appearance and I told him to tell Mr. Tear that it was a lion carrying off a deer, and to come on after me. I kept the trail to my left and it was easily followed in the wet grass.

I was riding the Old Dun, the best horse I ever had, and I had my rifle, and over my shoulders a red Mexican blanket. I followed the trail about three hundred yards, and Mr. Tear came up, and said he had seen where the lion had caught the deer. Just then I lost the trail, and stopped short, for I had had the trail a moment before and knew it must be very near me. Mr. Tear rode off some thirty yards to my left and I said to him, "I have lost the trail, look out for it." He replied, "Well, here is the deer covered up with grass."

Just at that moment, I looked around on the ground to the right to my horse, for the trail, and there, not four feet from my horse's heels, lay the lion. He was as flat as possible. The end of his tail was moving slowly and he was looking me right in the eye. He was in the worst possible place for me to shoot at him, being a little behind me on the right. I moved straight to the front about twenty yards, and the lion crouched flatter than ever if possible, supposing, I imagine, that I had not seen him.

When I had gone about twenty steps I spoke to Mr. Tear and told him I was going to shoot and to look out for me. I took the red blanket off my shoulders and laid it across the Dun's neck, thinking if the lion sprang on us, that he might light on the blanket. The Dun stood as firm as a rock and I aimed just behind the lion's right fore shoulder. His head was partly turned from where I was standing on my horse. At the crack of the rifle, and it did not make as much noise as usual, the lion turned and made an awful leap directly towards me. I had no time to load, but came to a charge bayonets, without any bayonet, and cast a longing glance toward Mr. Tear. His horse was on its hind legs and the Lt. had both hands in his mane, so there was nothing to hope for from that direction.

The lion made a big jump directly toward me, and another of the same size would have brought him to me, but for some reason, as he struck the ground he turned sharp around and his next jump was from me. He ran about thirty yards and turned a somersault and laid still. I had by this time reloaded and I approached him carefully to give him another shot, if he attempted to get up, but he was dead. The bullet had entered his right side, went through his heart, and down his left arm and rested on the back of his left paw, just under the skin. From the slight noise of the explosion, I think the cartridge was defective, or it would have gone staight through the lion instead of coursing down the arm and stopping.

I went to examine the deer. It was buried partially under grass and an old branch of brush that the lion had broken off and put under it. The soft part of the abdomen had been torn out and eaten. On the deer's throat were four deep holes made by the tusks of the lion, but there was no sign that he had been clawed, unless he had clawed him in the abdomen.

The wagons had come up in sight, and I beckoned to the soldiers to come to us. They supposed of course that I had killed a deer, and no one stirred from the carriages.

The soldiers took the lion and the deer and carried them to the road. As I approached and they saw what had been killed all, ladies and officers, got out and took a look. As they were admiring the lion, Lt. Kendall, who was with me when I captured the Devil Fish remarked, "Well, Colonel, you beat all for catching big sardines and killing big squirrels."

The lion had evidently crawled up to a small herd of deer in the dark and stormy night and sprung on this one. The prints of the lion's feet in the soft earth were very distinct, and he had evidently not moved after he once fastened onto the deer's throat but the deer had thrashed around a good deal and torn up the ground in the struggle.

In 1908 Judge Williams related personal experiences

with the puma (or panther, or lion, as Major Bliss called it). The Judge also provides rich background information concerning the animal.

Like many other American animals, the puma suffered unbelievable misnomers when our English forefathers first encountered him on our shores. They labelled him "panther." In Europe, the animal most similar to our puma was named, panther. The European animal had borne the same name, identical to a letter in Greek, more than 2500 years before, and no other animal had borne it. If there was any attempt by the English settlers to give the American feline a distinctive name, either in English or by adopting an Indian name for it, I cannot recall it.

The Spanish name for the animal shows the same error. The Spaniards called it a "leon," just as they called the jaguar a "tigre," not because they were the same animals but because they bore some resemblance to those animals. A jaguar is a "tigre" yet to the common people of Mexico and South America. Only educated people call it a jaguar, but the puma is a "leon" to all Spanish-speaking people in Mexico to this day.

I am inclined to think that this Spanish name accounts for the origin of a theory which I have encountered at various times in the Southwest, viz: That a Mexican lion is a different animal from the panther. Among animals of this species which I have seen, I have never encountered enough difference sufficient to warrant this claim, and I have not found any supporting evidence for it in books on the zoology of our country. I suspect the name "leon" used by the Mexicans, has caused imaginative people to hunt for a difference where there was none.

The French picked up the word "cougar" for the animal from some Indian language which I have not been able to find, but it was probably of the Algonquin family. [Modern dictionaries say it got to the French from the Brazilian Indians through the Portuguese.] It has received only limited acceptance, but it is preferable to our own word, "panther," which is in common usage.

The word puma comes from Peru, from the same language which furnishes us originally the name "chaqui" for our "jerked" meat. It has been said to mean a shade of color in the original language, as well as an animal. If so, it has an analogy in our English language. It is well known that in old Anglo-Saxon the brown bear was known as a "beorn." In time and under the process of eternal change going on in languages, it developed into two words, the one "bear" meaning the animal — the other "brown" meaning the color which had characterized the animal. Some such history may now be hidden away, and inaccessible in the story of this word in the Quichua language.

The imaginations of speculative men in the early days of New World history led them to some wild and fanciful theories based on small foundations. One of these is almost a classic, and I shall relate it as apropos to my subject. The site of the story is in an early settlement of the Argentine country and runs thusly: During one of the many outbreaks of the natives, a post had been sacked and some Spanish women had taken refuge in a nearby forest, unarmed, and of course unprepared in every other respect. During the night they observed "tigres" prowling around, evidently preparing to attack them. They trembled in fear, expecting death from the "tigres" at any moment. Then there came on the scene some "leones" to make death doubly certain. After a time, the terrified women discovered to their astonishment, that the "leones" were acting as guards and were actually coming between them and the "tigres" to ward off the attack of the latter! The long night passed with the "tigres" advancing to attack and the "leones" fencing them off until the animals disappeared with the coming of dawn. When the women finally escaped, the story passed into the hands of some early annalist, and became a part of the early history of that country.

The story seems improbable to frontier settlers who are acquainted with the habits of these animals. To my knowledge, it is not supported by a single recorded instance under any similar conditions. If true, it might easily have been that the pumas were simply intending to appropriate the kill for themselves. Yet this was the foundation for a theory, which I think was advanced by Azara, that the puma was a friend to the human race and an enemy to the jaguar. The theory remained in considerable credit almost up to our day, and has received the comments of some distinguished scientists.

Though he is a bloodthirsty and voracious animal, it is true that the puma rarely attacks a man, even in the most desperate necessities of defense or hunger. This is so well known that it is looked upon by man as a most cowardly animal. This trait is thought to be the consequence of ages of contact between man and the beast, resulting in the animal being cowed. The cow, the pig, other domestic animals, the snake, the deer, the antelope, and feeble, timid wild animals will turn on man under certain kinds of stress. On the frontier, I have never heard of but one case when the puma attacked man and that was under peculiar circumstances which are in line with our general experience of the animal. As it opens a chapter of frontier life in the Trans-Pecos country of many years ago, I will relate the story as I heard it.

The incident was related to me by Juan Cano, Sr., and was believed to have occurred in the foothills of the Davis Mountains about sixty years ago. Cano's uncle had been taken "cautivo" (captive) by the Apache Indians when he was a small boy and had lived with them for some time — so long that he was not kept under guard. One day he and an Indian youth went out to hunt antelopes. They finally found some grazing in a small cove, clear of timber (for the antelope always keeps to the open country). The clearing lay between jutting rocky points covered with juniper, mountain oak and other scrub. Cano's uncle lay hid in this covert, while the Indian proceeded to stalk the antelopes. He donned an antelope skin with head and horns and moved slowly and cautiously into the open. When the attention of the antelopes was attracted to him, he put himself in the position of an antelope grazing; when the antelopes resumed their grazing he advanced a few steps, gradually and cautiously approaching them. In his hands he carried his bow and arrows, ready to use them when he drew closer to the herd.

Cano's uncle lay in the covert watching his friend's gradual approach to the game, ready to rush to his aid when the proper time came. He was suddenly horrified to see a large puma spring out of the thicket on the other side. In two or three rapid leaps he reached the Indian youth whose attention was riveted on the antelopes. Almost instantly, the lad was killed, before Cano's uncle could render aid. On the appearance of the white boy, the puma left his prey and disappeared in the underbrush. It was evident that the cat had been watching the antelopes, and further, that the Indian had simulated the appearance and movements of an antelope so well as to have deceived it. It had killed him thinking he was an antelope.

Many tales are recounted in this country which illustrate the inborn reluctance of the animal to face mankind. It is a very dangerous animal to the white man's herds and flocks and hence it is persistently hunted and killed. Because of its well known cowardice, the hunter takes chances with it which he would not take with a bear or another animal of equal strength or agility.

Many years ago I passed the fresh carcass of a puma lying in an open plain near a public road in Pecos County. The position of the body confirmed the story I was later told concerning the kill. It seemed that a cowboy, armed only with a pocketknife and the inevitable rope, was riding down this road when he caught sight of the animal in an open plain. It started to run. For a short distance, the speed of the puma equalled that of the pursuing horseman — but the animal has no endurance and cannot continue the tremendous speed with which it makes its first springs. Our knight on a cowpony was vigorously swinging his lariat. After a toss or two, he caught the puma. Perhaps he didn't have the tiger by the tail — but he certainly had a white elephant on his hands. The big cat was lunging furiously in every direction on the open plain, and the cowboy felt that it might turn on him at any moment. He naturally felt a bit insecure, facing an angry, frightened puma with a pocketknife. His alarmed horse was taking a very dim view of the entire affair. To turn the animal lose meant losing his nicely knotted, top quality manila rope. That could be considered only as a last resort. In this extremity he spied a tall Spanish dagger plant, and his plans were laid. He contrived to let the puma pass on one side of the plant, drawing it ever tighter, and managed to drag the unfortunate animal up to the plant and secure it there. Then he dismounted, and taking out his pocketknife he proceeded very leisurely, with proper discretion, to stab the animal to death.

About 20 years ago the Fielder brothers had leased four leagues of school land from Pecos County. The land lay on the Pecos River about 22 miles north of the present town of Langtry. This is rough country, particularly near the river. It is full of rocky canyons, caves and good hiding places for wild animals. In latter years this section was frequented by a German named Julius, who was famous as a hunter and the owner of the best pack of trained hounds in all this country. At the time of our story, the Fielder brothers were alone in their fight against destructive wild animals. They raised sheep, the most defenseless of all domestic animals, and their warfare was a perpetual day and night battle. While pumas were with them in all seasons, there were certain times in the year when they were present in extraordinary numbers. It was claimed that they migrated regularly, moving north out of Mexico in the springtime and back in the fall. The puma cannot travel or live far from water, and that section was one of great water scarcity except in the bed of the Pecos River. Therefore, this migration went up and down the river, thus giving them the full benefit of both passages.

Usually the Fielder brothers were armed, particularly during the season of migration. But one day during the time between migrations, one of the brothers was riding his range unarmed, and attended only by a couple of hounds. The hounds were trained to hunt pumas and when they struck a trail and raced off with keen yelps, he knew it was the fresh trail of a puma. He followed, wondering what he could do in case the animal was "treed," but hoping to find some way to cope with the situation. The dogs finally bayed it in a shallow cave on a hillside. The entrance was too narrow for the dogs to go in and stand any chance with the cat or drive it out. He tried throwing rocks in at it, but he could not drive it out, nor hit it in such a manner as to inflict any damage. Finally he thought of a plan which worked successfully. From a thicket of small trees he cut a stick ten feet long and to the end of this he tied his pocketknife, blade open. By using this as a lance, he finally killed it with repeated "jabs." The animal refused, to the last, to rush out in the face of man.

There are some wild animals which seem to have what I may term great vitality; that is the power to sustain great injury without losing much muscular ability up to the point of death. Others have a small amount of vitality. You may shoot at a cottontail rabbit and wound it only in a leg with one small No. 8 shot, and yet the animal will fall over apparently paralyzed and helpless. On the other hand, I have shot a jackrabbit — which is really a hare — through the heart with a Winchester rifle ball, and had it run off apparently unharmed for quite a distance before falling dead.

Though it is a species of cat, which is supposed to have nine lives, our puma belongs to the class of animals which possesses little vitality. Several years ago I killed one with No. 6 bird shot. Mr. S. A. Purinton told me that many years ago one of his Mexican herders was standing in his little A tent after dark peacefully cooking his supper. Hearing a noise behind him, he whirled and saw an enormous puma inserting his head between the door flaps. His appetite gone, the alarmed herder hurriedly grasped a stone from his hearth and flung it with all might at the animal in his doorway. It struck the cat squarely in the head and killed him. It would have taken much more than this to have killed a bear or even a javelina, as I once discovered to my detriment.

This cat has some peculiar habits. I think it will eat almost any kind of meat, fresh or "high" (high is the English use of the word as applied to meat). It doesn't disdain our polecat when the larder is low. But it has unmistakable preferences. It will not eat meat "high" when it can get fresh. Rarely does it feed more than twice on its kill. While it will kill cattle, it prefers sheep, and colts are a luxury. After the kill it commences to feast generally from the flank and on to the vitals, drinking all the blood it can find. When the puma is gorged, it hides the remains of the carcass. If the prey is light, it carries the carcass to a hiding place. The cat takes one end of the prey in its mouth and tosses the body over its shoulders and back. The tracks plainly indicate whether or not the puma is burdened with a carcass. The prints of the hind feet will be out of line with those of the fore feet. When the cat kills a heavy animal, it drags the carcass. Years ago I followed a drag trail and found the freshly killed body of a full grown buffalo which had been dragged for about a half mile.

Unless it is disturbed, the puma always attempts to cover its leftover prey. Sticks, brush and weeds are carried in the cat's mouth and placed over the carcass. In this area where there is not an abundance of such things, grass is generally used. The camouflage often leads one to believe the grass was pulled out by hand. The covering of the body by the cat must be serviceable to the animal in ways that are not generally suspected, for in this country covering with grass calls attention to the carcass rather than hides it. The cut grass wilts and changes color in a very short time, and so becomes noticeable in contrast with the fresh grass around it. I am satisfied that most of the animals which feed on carrion find their food by scent rather than by sight, and the covering, of course, does not obliterate the scent. In this country our three great scavengers are crows, buzzards and coyotes. The scent of a coyote is as keen as that of a hound.

If the cat gets no benefit by covering its prey from the scent of carrion hunters, why does it follow the practice? It would seem that it must benefit in some manner, for wild animals rarely have useless habits. In explanation of this, my friend, H. F. Stephenson, has a very ingenious theory. He has noticed buzzards standing around a covered carcass at a distance showing signs of uneasiness and evidently afraid to approach it. He believes that since the carcass is covered and hidden, the birds are reluctant to tamper with it for fear it may contain something dangerous. The outward appearance of the carrion is so different the scavengers may be frightened by it. That same effect may be produced upon the coyote, which is notoriously shy of anything which suggests a trap. In addition, it may be that the birds or coyote can also scent the cat and it may have a wholesome fear of that animal.

Even when it kills, the puma is rarely far from water. After concealing its prey it drinks, then seeks a cool shady hiding place where the satiated animal sleeps. A knowledge of this habit goes a great way toward the destruction of the animal, as it enables the hunter who finds the carcass to also find the malefactor.

Due to the persistent war waged against this animal by stockmen, one would expect its numbers to greatly decrease. Yet this does not appear to be the case. The animal was never a colonist; it does not settle in one spot for any length of time. A wild horse roams its customary range year after year unless driven from it by force; the cimarron made its home on one set of crags so long as permitted to stay there. But the puma is a hunter and must always go in pursuit of game, so it wanders from place to place during its whole existence. It visits us now almost as often as it did twenty years ago. Due to the lack of surface water, the cat never frequented that part of our county which I have designated as the great dry divide, except in rainy seasons. Although that section is now watered by wells, it is still relatively free of pumas. The feline slinks up the Pecos River and steals out along our small tributaries and near our springs very much as it did in past years. Each year we hear of its depredations as frequently as ever. However, it may easily be that its appearances are not so frequent as in former years. Perhaps we make much more ado and give more publicity to its raids today than we did in times when settlers were sparse, and the attacks of beasts were taken for granted and endured silently.

The color of the puma is well suited to the prime object of its existence — the stalking of other animals. It is as valuable to the animal as the very similar color of the deer is to that animal. Nature has aided both animals, the hunter and the hunted, with the same device for concealment.

For purposes of concealment, our soldiers are now clad in khaki, but not half so effectively as the puma. The shade of difference in our khaki-colored uniforms makes them more similar to the Old World lion. Perhaps Old World soldiers should adopt this shade for uniforms. Nature has selected the puma's color after a process of thousands of years of trial. The animal uses the color effectively from Canada to Patagonia, in plains, forests and mountains. I think we may safely consider the verdict of nature to be that this is the color best suited in the New World for purposes of offensive concealment.

The Judge had a personal experience with a puma he did not include in the 1908 articles. In 1901 or 1902, it was written in a letter from Fort Stockton to his young daughter, Kathryn, who was living with her grandparents, the Jesse C. Williamses of Carthage, Illinois, while attending school.

About 30 miles northeast of here lies a remarkable hill which we may as well call the "Livingston Mesa." I use the Spanish word "mesa," because it describes the type of hill in a way superior to any English word I know. It means a hill with a level, flat surface. Such hills are not uncommon in this arid country —

but are very uncommon in other areas where rainfall is considered normal.

To the north of this mesa lies the broad, low valley of the Pecos River. The view from any point in the valley makes one think of some fortification thrown up by giants. The flat level surface runs here, into a well simulated bastion; and there into an entrant curve, while the detached remnants of the mesa make up the forts of redoubt. Reaching high into the southern sky, the long, craggy rampart is visible from a distance of 30 miles or more to the north of the river.

To your mother this mesa is chiefly notable as being the home of the "pitahaya" cactus, where she has feasted on our desert strawberries after a long and wearisome climb to the rocky rampart. The boys are intensely interested in it because it is the home of our big game. The larger wild animals in this area must seek better hiding places than the low lying level plains afford. The great mesa with its rocky caves, crags and impassable cliffs offers the only safe refuge now that man — the implacable enemy — has invaded the country. There, the javelina [wild hog] loiters in the narrow crevices. The lobo [woods or great gray wolf] and the puma establish their lairs in the larger caves, or in the coverts of the chaparral where the buckeye, cedar, juniper and persimmon provide low, thick, shady hiding places — because they are dwarfed by drought — as the Japanese dwarf by art.

Before man settled the frontier, this mesa was as permanent a home as these larger animals could have. They stalked the deer and antelope for food; the caves provided shelter and refuge, while springs in the nearby valleys furnished them water. With the advent of man, the deer and the antelopes were destroyed and they must hunt new food. Man brought horses, cows and sheep which supplied new food — but he also brought dogs and guns with which to protect his flocks. The mesa was no longer a safe home. Chased from place to place, the puma and the lobo became Ishmaelites — wandering forever — outlaws in the domain over which they had once reigned as chiefs. When evidence of their presence was spotted, baying hounds panted hot on their trail, horses thundered over the turf and shots echoed across the plains. They were denied rest until they were killed or driven away. Pumas are now rarely seen in this country. Due to its superior sagacity and speed the wily lobo still manages to exist here, though it is constantly hunted and trapped.

Last August I was on this mesa with Mr. Stephenson, Mr. Hock and two Mexicans. We were in this area on horseback. An early morning rain had conditioned the ground for easy trailing, so the hounds were following us. The motley crew was young and untrained, with one cur and two half-breeds. The only dog on which we could rely to do expert trailing was a sturdy old black and tan hound. Throughout the morning they had exhausted themselves racing after rabbits and small game. Around noon, when we turned our horses back toward the ranch, the only credit due the dogs was that they had startled a large wildcat — which they allowed to escape.

As we were slowly riding back on the crest of the mesa, I heard an exclamation behind me from a Mexican. Looking back, I saw a herd of 14 antelopes running toward us from our rear in that vacillating erratic manner peculiar to them. They ran a short distance in one course apparently following one leader, when without seeming cause they changed course and raced after another leader. They came on in zig-zag irregular fashion, until they passed within 60 yards in one of their tangential moves. We had no guns, so they passed in safety. Our Mexicans, with lassos looped dashed after them, spurring their horses to top speed, while the whole pack of hounds with yelps and barks took up the chase.

While gazing after the fast disappearing melee of dogs, horses and men, I heard Mr. Stephenson call. He was near a juniper bush examining the ground while beckoning to us. We approached the spot on which his gaze was focused, and at first glance I thought a few handfuls of grass had been pulled up and discarded under the shadow of the juniper bush. Closer scrutiny revealed the carcass of a four or five month old calf under the wilted clumps of grass. It lay in small bunches over the carcass precisely as though a man had uprooted it and used his hands to spread it over the body.

The moist ground showed signs of a struggle and of a body being dragged a short distance. The great cat-like track along the margin of the trail gave the culprit away. "A puma," Mr. Stephenson remarked sententiously. It was reasonably plain from the signs and tracks that a puma had hidden in the juniper bush until an unsuspecting calf had strayed near. With a sudden spring the puma had seized his prey and killed it. After eating out of the vitals it had dragged the calf into the bush and covered it intending to come back to it again. With the keen-eyed sopilote [turkey buzzard] soaring above in search of carrion, it was necessary to hide his prey, or, when our cat returned to feast again, he might find nothing but scattered bones for his banquet. The puma is never satisfied with one meal from his victim; he must have two or more if the carcass will furnish that much, and he lies in hiding nearby between meals. Armed with that knowledge, we naturally considered the line of bluffs not far distant to the south. The trail going away from the body led toward this line of bluffs at a point where the high mesa plain dropped over a wall of perpendicular rock down 60 or 70 feet into the head of a small but deep canyon running up from the lower plain well into the high mesa.

While slowly and carefully following the trail, Mr. Hock gave us a short chapter on the effect of the puma's device of hiding its prey. "Do you know," said he, "that the buzzard and the coyote are afraid to disturb a body that has been covered by the panther, whether the panther be in sight or not?"

"I have seen buzzards standing around a panther's cache," Hock continued, "in a circle and at a distance. At times one of them would advance toward the hidden carrion a short distance, when all at once with a curious cluttering it would jump backward with uplifted wings as if threatened with a stroke, and retreat to its companions. And until the panther finally abandoned its prey no buzzard would venture even to pick at the hidden body."

The trail led on over gravel and rocky ground, and we soon lost it. The Mexicans and the dogs returned from a fruitless chase after the antelopes, and with the aid of the dogs we kept up our course to the head of the small canyon. Here, on the very brink of the precipice — just where the curve of the canyon was at its most advanced point — we again saw a puma track. Looking down from the canyon walls at this point we caught sight of a fine tank of water — "tinaja" as the Mexicans would call it — 60 feet below us in the rocks. Beneath us the canyon spread into a veritable amphitheatre, with a semi-circle of rock wall, perpendicular and smooth, from the bottom of which the surface descended in a rapid graduation, broken by huge stones and dense thickets of shrub, to the water course in the middle. It was an ideal covert for our puma, and we concluded at once that he must be there. However, we could not find another one of his tracks on this canyon rim, search as we might. Our puma seemed to have vanished where his last visible track lay. We could find no place in the rocky wall where anything could descend. Yet, if we were to depend upon our dogs, the evidence indicated that he had not been on the rim, but a few steps beyond that track. We concluded that somewhere down that apparently impassable wall the agile puma had discovered a passageway which our eyes had not detected.

To test this conclusion we began detaching great rocks from the canyon walls and tumbling them down into the amphitheater below. These rocks would fall sheer, 60 feet before striking, and after landing would go crashing down the incline, splintering on rocks, crushing the scrub, and making enough noise to frighten ghosts if there were any in that dark turmoil of rock and bush. But our puma was too sly and cautious to rush out from his hiding place and we soon realized that if he lurked there, we could only find him with the help of our dogs.

We were compelled to lift the dogs from rock to rock by hand to lower them into the canyon. The old black and tan hound, the hero of our story, was lifted down also. I was stationed at the top of the canyon wall in a favorable spot overlooking the amphitheatre in order to detect any movement the puma might make to escape. From my perch I could see two of the dogs running in a random, flighty manner from place to place, often covering the same ground two or three times, gradually working off down the canyon and away from the amphitheatre. Not so with the old black and tan. With nose close to the ground and his tail wagging vigorously, he was slowly and carefully making his way up the canyon toward me, crossing from side to side in a systematic way in order that no ground might escape him. He was plainly an old veteran, and it was delightful to watch him. I had great hope that he would soon uncover our cat.

Just as he had reached the thickest of the underbrush, not far from the head of the canyon, the yelps of other dogs broke the stillness. Out from the bushes and on to a great protruding rock sprang the veteran. For a moment he stood there on one forefoot with the other uplifted while he listened. Then, as the yelps made it plain that the other dogs were in full chase, he dashed off down the canyon to join them. As quickly as I could I followed around the canyon rim only to find that our dogs had taken off in pursuit of a jackrabbit. This was very disappointing! By this time most of the party had become convinced that the puma was not in this canyon, but had passed on to the next canyon to lay down and spend the day. With difficulty, the hot, tired dogs were recalled from their useless chase. There were no air currents in the canyon and the heat was almost unendurable, so we proposed to let our dogs rest. The intense midday sun beat upon the exposed rocks until the radiation was like the blast from an open furnace.

While we were resting, Mr. Hock set out at once with the dogs which had not been down in the canyon. He missed the closing scenes of our chase. I was not satisfied with the search of the amphitheatre, so I climbed down into the canyon to seek the spot near the head, which had been left unexplored when the cry of the other dogs had disturbed the black and tan hound. The enormous rocks tilted in all directions and full of hidden caves. I suspected strongly that I was on the proverbial "wild goose" chase, rather than a puma hunt. With such an abundance of coverts and caves, the puma could lie within 10 feet of me, and I would never be the wiser. As I wormed my way back under the rock wall toward the place of descent, the area under a small juniper tree caught my attention. The tender grass lay pressed to the earth in an oblong space such as might have been occupied by the body of a puma when lying down.

I could find no tracks, but I did find some small gray hairs such as might have come from a wolf, a deer, or a puma. This was not a certainty, but it was such a probability that I raised the best imitation I could of the yell, "Yee-Hoee!" and brought the party toward me. The veteran hound was brought up and at once took up the trail of some animal, winding off in a serpentine course through the undergrowth. From his actions it was clear that he was on a very fresh scent.

Mr. Stephenson, as Master of the Hunt, ordered me to take up my station above on a projecting point of the canyon wall so that I might watch the movements of the puma when he was driven from his lair. I scrambled up and had barely reached the appointed spot when I heard the deep yelp of the hound. Feeling keen, vivid excitement, I searched the amphitheatre, but was unable to locate the dog. He gave a higher yelp and appeared on a large rock near the center of the canyon. A long, lean, reddish-yellow form projected into the air from a clump of dwarfed buckeyes, and our chase was on. Even in the excitement, I was struck by the leonine aspect of the animal while in the leap. For the first time I gave due credit to the propriety of the Mexican name for the animal, "leon." The small round head of the puma breaks the resemblance, but in the other outlines it is very strong.

The puma reached the foot of the canyon wall opposite to me in a few leaps and disappeared in a long fronted cave of shallow depth. The dog, spent and worn, with his red tongue lolling far out of his mouth, followed slowly. He entered the cave at one end, and the puma instantly shot out the other end. The cat trotted leisurely along a rocky ledge with the canyon wall on one side, and the steep, shrub-covered decline on the other. He began leaping from ledge to lower ledge and finally landed in the center of a juniper thicket and lay down in the shade. By following along above him on the rim of the canyon wall I was able to locate him as he went into this hiding place.

Our old veteran black and tan hound was very warm and very tired. As he slowly trudged up the trail, that long flame-red petal of tongue made a vivid picture against the background of white rocks and the black and tan body. But he was determined, and at regular intervals he gave a hearty yelp. When he reached the spot where the puma had leaped from the rocky ledge he missed the trail, and came slowly back to pick it up again. I came to the poor old weary fellow's aid. I threw some rocks down into the clump of junipers where the puma was taking his leisure. One of them must have struck the animal, for he bounded out with his usual high leap, and continued his course along the foot of the wall. The falling rocks attracted the dog's attention and he caught sight of the puma and took up the chase again. Footsore and hot, our hound traveled slowly and soon lost sight of the puma. Poor old black and tan staggered across a little water in a rock pool and he lay down beside it resting while he lapped it up to slake his thirst.

I followed the puma's course by staying along the winding escarpment of the wall top. Occasionally I lost sight of him, then he would reappear at some exposed point below me. I finally got well ahead of him and placed myself on a jutting point where I was certain to see him if he continued in his present direction, and here I waited. From this spot, I could see that Mr. Stephenson had left the canyon, reached the mesa, and was now mounting his horse to follow me. I saw the Mexican, Eduardo, far below in the canyon shrub, signalling to me that the puma had stopped at a point back along the bluff. I left my jutting crag and went back along the wall until I understood from Eduardo's gestures that the big cat was below me. However, I was unable to see him, nor could I see or hear anything of our dog. Mr. Stephenson had now come up, and I left him on the watch above, while I climbed down to discover the whereabouts of our game.

In the canyon wall near me there was a breakdown which I was able to climb. As I neared the bottom, I found myself just above a narrow vertical slit running back into the wall, and I took the easiest way down, dropping into the opening at the mouth of the slit, which was about five feet wide. As I landed, I cast a glance into the rift, and was not a little surprised to see the puma sneaking back into the dark end of the cave. I was completely unarmed, without even a pocketknife. As I stood contemplating my best course of action, he turned and came toward me with a curious swinging gait, evidently wanting me to get out. I knew that the longer I held him in the cave the better our chance to bag him, as our dog would be slowly drawing near. So I planted myself squarely in front of the narrow opening, waved my hat and yelled at him.

The bluff succeeded and back he went into the darkness. Only a moment later however, I saw him coming again, and again I bluffed him back. For the third time he turned and came toward me. This time I thought I detected a determined gleam in his eye, for he came at full speed with no sign of hesitation. Taking note of his attitude, my manners improved, and I politely stepped to one side, hugged the wall, and mentally drank "speed" to the parting guest. To my great satisfaction, he passed by without any attempt at a stroke at me, but I caught a whiff of absolutely foul breath. It had no suggestion of attar of roses I can assure you! If, at any time, I had had any pang of conscience about hunting to the death a wild animal which had done me no harm, I am certain that that whiff could have blown it to the winds. Any animal that carries such a breath might also carry the plague.

Again he traveled the foot of the cliff, followed at a distance by the dog which had resumed the chase. I was coming along still further behind, when I saw the panther in great leaps climbing up the perpendicular wall of the canyon some 300 yards ahead. I yelled a warning to Mr. Stephenson up above. From the clatter of the horse's hoofs and the yells which echoed, I was satisfied that he had spotted our cat and had given chase. As the hunt now seemed about to be carried to the mesa, I began to climb up the wall, and was surprised to see the hound struggling, with immense difficulty, up the same path the puma had taken. Reaching the top, nearly exhausted, I could neither see nor hear anything of the hunt. All was quiet and nothing could be seen of our actors. Following the wall some 300 or 400 yards however, I found Mr. Stephenson, dismounted, and looking down into the canyon.

Stephenson told me that the puma had gone over the wall again after a short but warm chase. Our old faithful hound had followed him, but was now lying under the shade of some bushes to recover from the heat. The puma, finding himself no longer pressed, was also lying down under a shrubby buckeye bush, which Mr. Stephenson pointed out to me.

We had a consultation. It was clear that our dog must be rested before he could work again. None of the other dogs had been on the trail for the last two hours, and were now up on the mesa with us. We could get them down, and start up our game again, but they had shown no skill in tracking and we were afraid that they would lose his trail and let him get away. If we could only hold matters in hand as they then stood until our black and tan hound could recover his wind, then we might hope for success. But to start the puma again at this time seemed to be folly. So we decided to wait.

It had been about three hours since the Mexican had started after the gun, and surely he must soon return. [The party was without any firearms when it discovered the puma's kill. The Mexican had been sent to the ranch house for a gun.] We waited on that bare rim rock with the sun beating straight down on us, and our eyes glued to that clump of dwarfed buckeyes. I was indeed glad to rest, for I was almost as much used up as the old black and tan, but I wasn't getting any cooler sitting on the white rock with the heat descending on me from the sun above, and rising from the rocks beneath. After about half an hour of waiting, during which neither the dog, nor the panther moved, the Mexican galloped up, his grey horse in a lather, and the gun across his saddle.

Mr. Stephenson handed me the gun as I started down the wall — and I was shocked! "Why," said I, "It's a shotgun! And these are No. 6 shot!" "It is alright," said he, "just shoot and keep a-shooting. We mustn't let him get away." To this I made no reply. I had very considerable confidence in Mr. Stephenson's skill and experience in puma hunting, but I must say that that confidence was undergoing a very heavy strain just then, when I thought of peppering that animal with those little shot which we do not consider heavy enough for our blue quail. But it seemed to be a groundhog case, "that or nothing," so I went on down, gun in hand, strongly suspecting those No. 6 shot would get me in trouble. Behind me I heard Mr. Stephenson and the Mexican trying to get two of the mongrels down the bluff.

As I went toward my game, I reflected that I must have a close shot in order for my No. 6 shot to have any serious effect. As I advanced nearer it occurred to me that the cat might take alarm and run off before I was in close range if it saw me advancing in a straight and undeviated line toward it. I moved to its left, hoping in this way the animal would be undisturbed until I got closer. Within 40 feet of its covert, I turned my steps abruptly to the right to pass to that side, which would give me, a right-handed man, a better chance to handle my gun. This took me over a smooth surface of solid rock on the right side of the buckeye bush and gave me an unobstructed view. Within about 25 feet of the bush, I caught sight of the puma's forepaws through an opening in the leafy circumference, then I saw his head resting on his paws, his eyes following my every movement. Instantly I threw my gun to my shoulder and fired.

When the smoke cleared I could make out the form of the animal landing from what must have been an unusually high leap. With satisfaction I saw that he landed in a stumbling manner as if one foot or both might have been injured. However, he dashed off across the mesa evidently headed for the high canyon wall on the other side. If he reached this, he stood a good chance of escaping, as our only effective dog seemed to be about used up and unable to work. I took after him, but before I had taken 20 steps, the old hound zipped past me with the two mongrels in hot pursuit. They were running fresh, while the cat was lame, and in a few moments they had our game bayed in a juniper thicket in the very center of the valley.

When I approached the bush I saw that he had on his fighting clothes. Like a skillful gladiator he had placed himself in position to fight to the best advantage. The thicket had only two openings through which the dogs could reach him, and he placed his back to the thickest of the bush so that the dogs could not rush him from behind, but had to face him through the openings on the right and left. The dogs wisely contented themselves with rushing in from the side for a short nip and leaping out again. The great cat was the picture of rage with his ears flattened against his bullet-like head, his yellow eyes wide open, revealing only a narrow black pupil, and his large, sharp teeth exposed in an angry snarl under bloody nostrils. As I approached, he changed fronts to face me, but didn't falter in his battle against the dogs, but he used his paws only in striking. One unfortunate dog wasn't fast enough and was knocked fully 20 feet. He took off running, apparently very frightened, but not hurt.

I waited some time for the dogs to be out of range, then fired a snap shot at his head just below and back of the ear. I was not twenty feet distant, but the only apparent effect was to cause a sudden and vicious lunge toward the dogs. I began to think over my original presentiment about the No. 6 shot with a good deal of disgust, for I was certain I could not have missed him — but in a few minutes I fired again aiming as before, and the animal fell over on its side, and died almost without a struggle. The dogs rushed in and you would have thought from the fury with which they tore into the puma that they were the bravest and most ferocious animals in creation. Yet had it arose again they would have been away in the twinkling of an eye to return to their Fabian policy. But this puma would move no more.

That evening we carried home a puma skin, two teeth, some claws, and some tallow, which our Mexican claimed was an infallible cure for rheumatism and diverse other maladies to which human flesh is heir. These mementos are proof of our puma hunt. If you require proof of the powers of tallow, Eduardo will point out his right leg which he claims was cured of rheumatism by this same tallow, and in his mind there cannot possibly be better proof.

About seventy-two years after Judge Williams' experience with the panther on the Livingston Ranch, I was getting Tom Moore's stories about his hunting dogs. Tom told me that he was about thirteen years old at the time the foregoing story occurred and had been present at the killing of that panther.

I had quit school. Old Professor Hobbs was pretty tough on us so I ran off from school and never went back. I got a job at the Livingston Ranch. A puma had killed a calf. Our dogs trailed the puma three or four hours along the bluffs. Finally he [the puma] went into a cave back in a bluff.

Well, we didn't know what to do for the dogs couldn't go in there, because when they did the puma would slap them and they would come out of there. We decided the best way to get him out was to get someone to go in there and run him out. We had with us "Hijo" [Eduardo] Gonzales, Mac Garcia, Tom Mooney, Hiram Stephenson, Col. Ike Hock, Morgan Livingston, and Judge Williams. When none of the others volunteered to go in, finally Judge Williams said he would.

He took a lantern with him as he kept close to the sidewall of the cave and looked ahead. The roof of the cave was so low that he was bent over and couldn't straighten up. It [the puma] was about thirty or forty feet back. He soon saw the puma's eyes looking at him [as reflected by the lantern's light]. When he got close enough that the puma could see the floor under the light, it ran out. We all were holding the dogs and seeing what was going on. When Judge Williams yelled, "Here he comes!" that puma came out of there and everybody fell over backwards getting out of the way.

As Tom's story differs a little from that of Judge Williams, I suggest that a lapse of seventy-two years could obliterate many details in anyone's mind.

The Judge's two older children wrote their recollections of incidents concerning pumas on or near the Williams ranch on the Pecos in the 1890s. Ermine Garnett wrote:

On cool mornings I loved to ride through a fairly large draw lying between our ranch and the Ray ranch. The draw, with its numerous large mesquite trees was an ideal nesting spot for mockingbirds. I have very vivid recollections of the incomparable music of these songbirds as I rode my roan pony along this wooded area. This was called Panther Draw because panthers (or pumas) were sighted in the area on numerous occasions. I frequently noticed puma tracks in the road as I passed through.

I remember one incident which was typical of Panther Draw. A Mexican named Bonifacio worked on our ranch and kept a saddle mare and his black mule close to his house. He was awakened one night by a noise in the corral. He went out, but darkness obscured whatever activity had occurred. Early next morning he found the tracks of a large puma and evidence of a fight between the puma and the mare. The mare's colt was gone, and both the mare and the mule were badly scratched but not seriously injured. When he reported this to the ranch, the whole neighborhood was aroused, the dogs were gathered, and a puma hunt was started which lasted over a period of several days. Apparently the puma had leaped over the fence with the colt on his back, then dragged it some distance where he killed it, fed on part of it and covered the remains with grass. A pack of hounds was brought over from the Carr ranch but after trailing the puma for several days, mostly back and forth across the Pecos River, the trail was finally lost.

Ermine and her older brother frequently spoke of a puma hunt on the river when Gene Sweat, afterward a county judge of Ward County, was a nine-year-old boy. Not long after Bonifacio's colt was killed, dogs were gathered from the NA Ranch and a puma hunt was launched on the river.

The dogs were hot on the trail of a puma when Gene and his father were crossing the river. Gene's father wanted to get in on the excitement and had hurried ahead of Gene, as the boy was looking for "boogers" on all sides. Gene was all alone astride his horse when he saw the puma cross the Pecos just below him. In a loud cry he called out, "Hey! Somebody come here. I'm lonesome!"

Concerning his experiences with pumas from 1930 to the present, Charlie Stone said:

> I've caught only four pumas in my life and I wasn't trapping for them then. They were caught in No. 4 Newhouse traps, which held them fine. I had dogs with which we followed the trail of the dragged trap. When we came to the pumas in the trap, we just shot them. A puma will eat deer mostly but it eats rabbits, goats, sheep, colts and burros. The puma drug those traps about two or three hundred yards and then the hooks on the chains got caught in the

brush. The reason why trappers use hooks is because if they just tied it to a bush or something the animal might just then pull out or get his foot or toes cut off and escape. If you put a hook on the end of the chain connected to the trap, they'll drag it a ways and get it caught on a bush. By that time the trap has dug deep into the foot or leg.

Some people use bloodhounds to trail pumas. A bloodhound has a lot better scent than a Walker hound. But a Walker's much faster on the trail.

Panthers have their cubs on a boulder up on a big rock or on a mountain above a canyon. A panther has to have water.

From lofty elevations, the puma looks down and spots its intended prey at water holes. The crafty animal slips down within close range, crouches for a quick spring, and races after its meal. For a distance of about two hundred yards, it is the fastest animal in the country. The antelope, which can run about fifty miles an hour, often falls prey to the swift puma.

The antelope's curiosity is legendary — even the pumas are aware of it. The big cat will crouch, raise its tail, and wag it, while the antelope comes closer and closer. When he's close enough, the puma charges and often catches an antelope.

In the beginning of this chapter, the prey of Zenas R. Bliss' panther was a deer. Just recently, Bill Carrol, an employee on the great E. L. spread, south of Fort Stockton, told me he had seen a panther on the western extremity of the ranch. Although pumas are seldom seen in this region now, there are many antelopes on the E. L. Ranch, for it's a game preserve.

A predatory puma was killed on the P. C. Coates ranch, east of Fort Stockton, not more than a year ago. It required the use of trained dogs and took the combined efforts of a group of ranchers to hunt that animal down — but not before it had killed hundreds of dollars' worth of livestock.

The Bear (Black)
The Genus Euarctos Americanus

"Algie met a bear; the bear was bulgy; the bulge was Algie."

It behooves man to walk softly, quietly and very cautiously around these furry denizens. They can be temperamental and totally unpredictable. In 1908, Judge Williams had done considerable research on bears.

> We have heretofore been writing about animal characters which rejoice in a Christian name only. Their names do not indicate that they are legitimate members of any family. . . . The bear carries a family

name, and a "tree" with duly registered branches. . . . We do not hear of "Polar" or "Black" or "Brown" or "Grizzly," but we have a full baptismal name, given with the sanction of science. It is "Polar Bear" or "Black Bear" or "Brown Bear" or "Grizzly Bear." It is the house of "Bear," and the surnames follow as a matter of rightful heritage. . . .

America may be the home of bears, but this particular part of it 'yclept' [named or called] Pecos County has not been one of the animal's favorite haunts. I believe we have been completely free of "Old Ephraim." During the past 25 years I have heard that grizzly bears have been killed in the Davis Mountains, 70 miles west of us. Certainly some large bears have been killed there. Throughout those years I have never heard that such an animal was killed in this [Pecos] county. I am inclined to believe that the large bears killed in the Davis Mountains belonged to the variety known to the [local] Mexicans as "platados," and to Americans as "silver tipped." Thirty years ago this variety was said to be found in the mountains in Arizona, New Mexico and Old Mexico. Twenty-eight years ago, on San Francisco Creek in Arizona I saw some skins of this kind and noted the great size and the white tipped hairs of the animal. Around seven years ago I had planned to go into the mountains across the Rio Grande, south of us, with Dr. Phillips of the State University to hunt "silver tips." We had received information indicating that they were fairly abundant there. As we did not go, my information remains now as it was then, purely hearsay.

The "platado" has not made his home in Pecos County. Our county is the habitat of the black bear. Along the Pecos River below Sheffield and around the mouth of Independence Creek, this bear found a congenial home. For a number of years, both the shin oak and live oak provided mast (the fruit of these trees); there were plum thickets; there were the roots of the Indian Bread (psoralea); if fortunate, he could revel in honey from the hives along the bluffs; and he had abundant thickets of low brush and rock caves in which to hide.

Out on the open prairies, on the great dry divide, the bear was not at home. For him, it was not what Mowgli called "good hunting." Thirty years ago, and perhaps always, the bear was rarely found on plains. I shall never forget my astonishment at an apparent exception to this rule in 1878. On the level floor of the Llano Estacado I discovered the carcass of a black bear. As far as the eye could see there were no bushes and no vegetation excepting the low clumpy grass which is a peculiarity of that country. It is a fine country, but I have never seen land more destitute of plant life. I could not speculate what might have brought this animal to such a place. However, we had not traveled another mile until we came to the Palodura (Hardwood) Canyon, one of the most remarkable canyons, which it has been my privilege to see. Cut by the process of erosion for miles back into a high, smooth, level table land, this canyon was 300 to 400 feet deep and covered with nothing but grass. The sides from top to bottom were cloaked with "piñones" and cedars, but not a single tree grew from the canyon's edge out into the high plateau. There were many black bears in this canyon, and I presume the carcass I saw was that of an unfortunate animal which had strayed away from his native bowers.

In spite of its clumsy, awkward appearance the animal is so quiet and cautious in its movements that it is rarely seen, except when it wanders into country unfavorable to hiding. Often the only proof of his presence is that telltale track, so like and yet so unlike the human foot. Several years ago one of these animals stopped at what is known as the Middle Well on the Livingston ranch near the Pecos River, and went fishing in the tank. He succeeded in catching a good sized carp and evidently was not very hungry, as he was particular enough to reject the head and the bony tail. Although there were six or eight cowboys riding the range every day, and the well was only two miles from headquarters, no one saw that bear. If not for the telltale tracks around the tank, no one would have been able to identify the fisherman.

Bears evidently do a lot of migrating and wandering. They never hibernate in this section. Twenty-five years ago it was rumored that they migrated at regular seasons every year in and out of the mountains around Fort Davis. This may have been true. Evidently the animal has a migratory instinct, otherwise it is difficult to account for its appearance in certain places at certain times. About three years ago one appeared on the high road about one-half mile north of Fort Stockton. No prodigal that roamed over the great dry divide was more "lean, rent and beggared by the strumpet wind." His undernourished ribs were painfully plain; patches of hair had fallen out and that which remained was dry and withered. The animal was decidedly seedy. He had probably wandered off his course in migrating and had passed over some of the Pecos County dry country. Our Nimrods dashed out with dogs and guns to hunt him down, but Mr. Bear hadn't seen a welcome mat in the first place — he was gone and was never seen again.

Other people had experiences with bears in the Trans-Pecos region. My friend, Charlie Stone, related the following:

> A bear's an old son-of-a-gun. He will kill cattle or sheep. It's a scavenger animal. I never did kill a bear in Pecos County, but I've killed some in the Davis Mountains. I usually just took a bunch of dogs and jumped them [bears] and shot 'em. Chase them up a tree or something.
>
> One time I was trapping at Mr. McCutcheon's Ranch in the Davis Mountains when a fellow rode by and said he'd seen where a coyote killed a couple of sheep over there by Chalk Springs, so I told him I'd go see about it. I saddled up a horse, put some traps on my saddle and headed out. When I got about there, I crossed an old creek and went over a bluff to where an old bear had killed those sheep and was still eating on one.
>
> When he saw me, he really took out of there through a catclaw thicket. So I went ahead and dragged

that old dead sheep up between some catclaw bushes so that he'd have to go through them to get to the sheep on one side or the other. I set two traps, one on each side of the sheep, and went on back to the ranch.

The next morning I took my old dog and went back up there. I knew I was going to catch that bear. Sure enough, I had caught him in a trap and he had dragged it off. My dogs really took to that bear's trail which went four or five miles up a big canyon. I had to go way around on horseback to get above the upper part of the canyon. There I got off my horse on the hill above the canyon and came down that mountain afoot. I walked down and sat on a big old high bluff.

Then I hid among those rocks when I heard those dogs baying as they were coming closer. I sat there awhile and pretty soon that old bear came right up that canyon. When he got down right under me I shot him in the back of the head right behind the ear, and killed him.

In about two or three minutes those hounds got there and boy they really tore into him. He was already dead but they really chewed and clawed him.

My companion, Ray Phillips, rode up about that time. I said, "Get off your horse and help me load this bear on my horse." He said, "I'm not getting off my horse cause it's scared to death of that bear." I said, "Well, come on down here and help me get him on my horse, 'cause I can't load him myself."

I rode down there and my horse never did scare or nothing and I rode right down there by that bear. So I tied the bear's feet up and pulled him up on the saddle. I took him back to the ranch and Mr. McCutcheon said, "That bear sure is fat. I'm going to eat him." The cook skinned the bear and fed it to the sheep-shearing crew that was there.

No bears ever stay in Pecos County much because bears live in caves and mountains and there are not many in Pecos County.

Old man Casey's daughter, Thelma, always wanted a baby cub bear. I told her if I ever caught one I would bring it to her. A little while after that she got married to a cowboy who was working there. Afterward, he jumped an old sow bear and two little ones. The little ones were about the size of housecats.

He got off his horse and chased the cubs until he caught one of them. About that time here comes that old sow, charging him. He dropped that bear cub and ran to a little piñon tree. The first limb was about six or seven feet above the ground. He told me right then it didn't look very tall to him. He made it up past it with no trouble at all, considering what was behind him. The sow didn't try to climb up after him.

She got her cubs and went on her way. He told me he stayed up in that tree till the bears had made it all the way around the mountain.

These were all black bears. I've seen one that was killed on Jim Buckly's that when he skinned the hide out it was as big as a black mulley heifer. I figure that bear weighed four or five hundreds pounds. That bear was killed in 1938 or 1939. A bear will catch a cow by the hindquarter and just take a hunk out of the cow while it's running.

Another friend, the late Henry Wilbanks, of Fort Stockton, related two of his experiences with bears in the Davis Mountains. On one occasion, he was working for a ranchman, and he rode up to a stock water tank where thirsty cattle stood around declining to drink for fear of a bear standing in the middle of the tank.

Henry threw rocks at it — ineffectually. The unperturbed bear held his position. My friend shucked his garments and waded within reach of the bear with the intention of shooing him. How he proposed doing this, I don't know — bears don't shoo easily, and this one was no exception. The bruin promptly slapped Henry under the water and continued to whallop him as fast as he could surface. Wisdom dawned on a groggy, water-logged Henry and he dived away and left the bear in possession of the tank.

Another time, while working for an extremely frugal

rancher, Henry was stationed in a line shack near the lower end of a canyon. The bossman ordered him to keep a hog in a sty in order to make use of what little food he might throw away. Although he was furnished with a rifle, only one cartridge was issued in order to discourage rifle practice.

News arrived that a bear was depredating in the region and Henry's boss trekked in to inform him that the dogs would start searching for the bear down the head of the canyon the following morning. Henry was ordered to go up the canyon and join the hunt at an early hour.

As Henry trudged up the canyon that morning, he heard the dogs, and the tone of their baying told him they had cornered the bear. Upon reaching the scene he found that his boss was not there, and it behooved Henry to dispose of the bear or lose his job. That one miserly cartridge must do the job. He took deliberate, careful aim, fired and to his dismay the uncooperative bear didn't drop dead, but remained very much alive, with only the loss of one eye. The bear was bent on escape whether Henry had more cartridges or not. He knocked aside a few dogs on his blind side and clumsily lumbered off as the dogs cautiously tantalized him.

Henry stated that he was more afraid of his Scrooge-like boss than he was of that bear. He removed his shoes so he might quietly slip up on the blind side of the bear, opened his pocketknife, and leaped on its back to escape those deadly claws. He reached under and cut its throat. Though Henry's knife slash was fatal to the bear, it managed to reach back and rake off the flesh all the way across Henry's chest, resulting in a scar that he carried the remainder of his life.

There is a site close to Sheffield, Texas, where a man was killed by a pet bear. Mrs. Lynn Bedell of Pecos County told me of her father's fatal experience with his pet bear. Her father, Mr. Tom Brown, operated a service station on the east outskirts of Sheffield, Texas. He had been given a bear cub by Mr. Brownrigg of Ozona and had bottle-fed it on milk, just as mothers feed their babies. When it matured it weighed about three or four hundred pounds. He kept it tied on a chain near the filling station to attract customers.

When my children were small I stopped at this station and the young ones wanted to be familiar with the bear. I wouldn't let them get near it for I was afraid of any kind of bear. Most wild animals, even if they are captured while small and fed on a bottle, retain many of their primitive instincts.

In the late 1930s, Mr. Brown took his family and the bear to his ranch-farm on Live Oak Creek, across the Pecos from Sheffield. He chained the bear to something under a highway bridge across from the ruins of old Fort Lancaster. Shortly thereafter someone reported that the bear had broken loose from its chain. Mr. Brown found his bear, but it charged him and bit and clawed him to death before anyone could stop it. No one knew what provoked the angry bear to such viciousness. Word was sent to neighboring ranchers, who formed a posse. The bear was found and killed the next morning not far from the scene of its master's death.

Prairie fires were a prevalent and dreaded danger to early settlers. When they got out of control, the consequences were devastating — not only to the settlers, but to the wildlife in the area. In the following paragraphs Judge Williams delivers a graphic treatise on the subject:

> Years ago the country was often devastated by great prairie fires. This was particularly the case in the southern and western parts of the county. I have known a fire to sweep the entire country from Leoncito Springs to the road running south from Fort Stockton to Haymond, a distance of 40 linear miles. The fires were more frequent and more destructive in the southern part of the county, near GH & SA railway. These early engines were imperfectly supplied

with spark arresters and often spewed forth sparks which ignited the dry grass.

Today, we have developed several methods of fire fighting and fire prevention. The steady influx of settlers has given us a larger population with which to fight fire. Many of them are willing to stand watch and guard against fire before it breaks out. In many places we have built fire guards by ploughing, and by cutting new roads which prove a great protection even in the event of high winds. The most efficient protection has resulted from natural causes. Our land is much more heavily stocked than in earlier times and the grass is kept closely cropped, consequently, a fire is more easily checked.

Our grasses do not generally grow thick enough to form a sod. We have a few flats in the county where the Toboso grass grows fairly close set. We also have a few places in flats and near the heads of coves in hilly country where mesquite grass grows fairly well set into a sod. In such places fire is difficult to control even now. But as a rule our land is set in varieties of grass, such as the grammas, which grow in sparse clumps from 6 to 12 inches apart with nothing between but bare ground. It would seem that in such country fire might be easily checked. Such is the case now.

In the days before the county was well settled, these grasses had been untouched by animals. We had no wild animals to consume them. The deer is a "browser" rather than a "grazer," preferring to pick the twigs and leaves of brush and to eat weeds rather than eat grass. About the only grass known to be eaten by antelopes is that found about prairie dog towns usually called "goose" grass. As a result of this condition, these sparse clumps of grass remained intact from animals, and only perished after years from a kind of dry rot, or when brittle and light it was broken off and carried away by the winds. On examination, a clump of grass would be found to contain not only the green grass of the current year, but also that of several previous years in various stages of dessication. This condition was highly favorable to the rapid spread of fire, and rendered it most difficult to check.

About 23 years ago [1885] a raging fire spread to the north from the railroad between Maxon Spring and Emerson. Its ugly scars slash across the face of the land to this day [1908]. It broke out under circumstances highly favorable for spreading. Unusual rainfall pelted down throughout the summer of 1884, and consequently we had lush stands of grass. The wet summer was followed by the "dry years" famous in our early history. For a long time south and southeast winds stealthily drew the moisture from everything on the face of the earth, only resting occasionally to let dust hurricanes from the north or northwest vent their anger on the parched earth. For months those sinister whirlwinds danced and gyrated across the land, spinning thin, snakelike lines of dust and withered grass far up into the sky. The color green had vanished from the face of the desolate earth, and vegetation neither blossomed nor flourished. The few flocks of sheep in the country had been driven to the Rio Grande, or their owners were in sore trouble and toiled for water and food to keep them alive.

Then a raging inferno crowned the suffering earth with a ring of flames. A passing engine on the railroad belched forth sparks near Longfellow — and the arid land was ignited. Section men on the railroad hurried to the scene, but they were too late. It was beyond their control. An east wind rapidly carried a long tongue of flame up the valley towards House Mountain, and south wind turned the column to the north. The ranches of Messrs. Purinton, Paxton and Downie lay 20 miles to the north in a line, facing the advancing wall of fire. A long front of rising smoke warned them of coming calamity. Fiendish whirlwinds danced high above the smoke, whirling a sinuous, writhing line bordered in black with the carbon skeletons of vanished grass. Tossing their home affairs into such condition as they could, the ranchmen hurried to meet the enemy before it reached the gates.

They found their efforts powerless. The fire had spread up to the hillsides, out of the valley, and hungry flames were licking toward a slope covered with sotol and lechuguilla. The flames would leap as high as 50 feet like the breakers on a rock-bound shore, while the constant popping of the sotol leaves sounded like the discharge of small arms in a battle. If the desperate fire fighters extinguished it in one spot, an eddy of wind would breathe new life to the embers; or live coals and embers would reset the flame. After consultation the fire fighters decided it was impossible for them to quell the mighty conflagration with their feeble force. They determined to confine their efforts to an attempt to save enough grass on which to carry their flocks until rain should bring new vegetation. By counterfiring, ploughing, and fighting the edges of the fiery torrent, they managed to save some plots of ground for the sustenance of their flocks. The fire swept over and around them, and on to the hills north of them. After several days, the wind changed direction and drove the fire back to the area already burned, where it died out.

Somewhere in the hills south of Big Canyon a bear lay in covert when the great fire advanced to the north. Perhaps it lay in some small juniper brake near Big Canyon where there was a well, else he could not have lived in there for lack of water. When the fire reached him, he must have made an attempt to cross through the flames. Blinded, burned and half suffocated, he struggled valiantly through the sea of fire and onto one of those plats of grass which the sheepmen managed to save from the flames. Here, the pitiful beast was found by a Mexican herder, rolling in agony in the dust, pawing at his eyes, as though to tear away some impediment to his sight. Mercifully, the herder killed him. He had made his last migration, and to him the end of the world had come by fire.

I have been told that a bear killed a man in the Sacramento Mountains west of the Pecos even though mortally wounded. During the elk-hunting season, one party of hunters had just killed and loaded an elk on their pickup when they heard a shot, followed by a man's scream. Within a few seconds they heard what they thought was an answering shot from the man's partner.

Later that night the radio announced that a hunter had shot a bear on the hill above him. Although mortally wounded with a bullet through his heart the bear rolled downhill past the man and tore most of the hunter's entrails out as he went by. When the hunter's partner got there, both the man and the beast were dead.

The Coyote
(Canis Latrans)

The controversial coyote, or prairie or brush wolf, is reportedly now active from northern Alaska to Costa Rica, having recently extended its range into the arctic regions despite its life of constant danger from man's vigorous attacks on it by means of traps, guns, poison and hunting dogs. Man's fight against the lobo, grizzly bear, and cougar or mountain lion has nearly exterminated the larger predators, but not the coyote. It eats anything that don't bite it first and some things that do!

In the late 1880s until 1900, sheepmen moved their

herds around over the Trans-Pecos country for free grazing. Seasonally, they traveled up and down the Pecos, summering in New Mexico and wintering on the lower Pecos. Charles Downie, Paxton and Purington found permanent locations in Pecos County and started their separate ranches in the early 1880s. All predatory animals were a scourge to them. Pens made of brush formed a night corral for the sheep and coal oil lanterns were strategically placed to keep the varmints away. A lone herder and his dog stood guard over the flock as it grazed during the day.

Both sheepherders and ranchers employed trappers and hunters, scattered in camps over their range to catch and kill lobos, coyotes, lynx and other predatory animals. In 1904, I rode horseback through a portion of the Downie ranch. North of his headquarters I came to a trapper's lean-to, where a hungry boy was served deer meat jerky with onions and potatoes. The trapper caught his own meat, but Downie supplied other necessities. The trapper's line of traps was supposed to protect the north limits of the Downie pastures. On the east side of Downie's pasture, I came to a camp which had dogs. They were fed only with mush, so their sense of smell and their appetite for meat would be keen.

Writing in 1908, the late O. W. Williams said:

> The name *coyote* has almost entirely superseded the old name of *prairie wolf*. The old name has a certain picturesqueness and propriety in it, not common animal nomenclature, and I regret to see it pass off the stage. The animal is certainly as much a "prairie" animal, as the antelope and the prairie dog, and in America, scenes of the prairies are almost inevitably accompanied by a picture of a coyote.
>
> In hunting for food, the patient, persistent coyote exhibits a certain kind of wisdom in "ways that are dark and tricks that are vain" — yet we do not credit it with even the slightest courage. It never faces an enemy of equal power, not even in defense of its

young. No masterless and friendless outlawed dog ever descends to the depths of sneaking, hiding, and cowardly cunning which characterizes this free wanderer of the plains.

But there is a method in his cowardice — the value of numbers appeals very much to his sense of fitness in the universe. The Mexicans say that a pack of coyotes will combine in a chase after some weaker animal, so that what could not be done by the unaided effort of one, is accomplished by the combined effort of many. I was once a witness to an instance which seemed to bear this statement out.

I had employed some Mexicans to clear a large piece of land for cultivation. We had quite a large space cleared, when I saw a coyote dash over the cleared ground in hot pursuit of a jackrabbit. As both animals passed close to us, we noticed the coyote seemed sluggish and lagged far behind, while the rabbit seemed to be very fresh and active. About half an hour afterwards, the rabbit, followed by a coyote, crossed the cleared ground again. After they had crossed, a Mexican told me that this was not the coyote that had first chased the rabbit over the open plat. I asked him how he knew, and he told me that the last coyote had a split, or badly cut ear. I did not consider this conclusive evidence, as both coyotes may have had a split ear. When the rabbit crossed for the third time, followed by two coyotes, neither of which had a split ear as far as I could see, I concluded that probably the Mexican was right. There was some evidence of teaming up between two coyotes, and there might as easily have been three or four in the combination. These combinations are probably among animals of the same litter, which have grown up and associated together.

Another observation of the Mexicans is that no one sees a coyote heavy with young. I am not aware of any explanation given by them for this fact. When I have inquired if Madam Coyote hid away out of shy regard for the proprieties, about the only reply I have had was "Quién sabe!" I am bound to say that my experience tallies with this observation by the Mexicans, for I have never seen a coyote in this condition, when the condition was noticeable.

If it is true that the animal is rarely seen in this condition, it can be reasonably explained. The coyote is a strict businessman, engaging in hunting to sustain life. He has no time for picnics and opera parties, but must exert his energy looking for the next morsel to nibble. He frequently encounters danger, and a coyote heavy with young would be at a great disadvantage, both to procure food and escape danger. It would lack speed, endurance and muscular coordination necessary to catch such game as rabbits, quail and prairie dogs, which it hunts in daylight. However, it might do some nighttime hunting, using its powerful sense of smell to locate concealed coveys of quail, or find nests. It might also track crippled or wounded animals. I am inclined to think that at this period of life, Madam Coyote avoids hunting by day, hunts a little at night, and probably exists on portions of prey brought to her by her partner. I have no evidence of this last conclusion. I simply offer it as a probable theory.

The Mexicans tell me that when you hear the staccato yelps of a coyote early on a summer morning just after sunrise, it will surely rain. There are many Americans who subscribe to this belief. I do not, but experience has shown me that it does often rain the day the coyote barks just after sunrise. (I do not like the word *barks* to describe the noise made by the coyote, but it is the current expression.) When there is moisture in the air, or atmospheric conditions suggest rain, the coyote indulges in the yelping cachinnation very early in the morning. I do not know why it chooses these particular conditions under which to play its lonely, forlorn sounding music, but I am satisfied it may be connected with a feeling of contentment. Perhaps it is a type of grace before a full meal, or a style of thanks afterward, for these times mean good hunting for the coyote.

The rabbits come out to drink after a long abstinence; lizards make their short spasmodic runs in every direction; insects come out of their hiding places; and indeed, the animal kingdom, both hunters and the hunted, is moved and agitated. The tarantula, the centipede, the rattlesnake and the coyote all come to the hunt. Not only is the prey more abundant, but the coyote can expect a keener and more vivid scent on the trail of its victims. To some extent, this condition exists in all temperate regions, but it is most noticeable in this semi-arid country. It appears that the animal kingdom is on a grand dress parade, preened for show, and each member exercises its keenest instincts, from the mockingbird warbling in the mesquite bush, to the rattlesnake slithering on the ground gazing at the singer with glistening and quivering tongues. The torpid tarantula stalks about on its high, stilted legs. The prairie dog busily cleans mud and trash out of its doorway, for these are an eyesore to this tidy housewife. The millipede comes out of its hole and pays its annual visit to its neighbor. Amid this carnival the coyote plays his role and adds cacophony that sometimes mars the occasion.

The coyote has a powerful sense of smell. I should think it is as strong as the hound or the pointer. The dog has been encouraged by man to cultivate this faculty for special purposes useful to man — but the coyote's very existence depends upon his ability to scent his daily food and nature has sharpened his scent glands to an extraordinary degree. For example, in the fall of 1886 I carried a survey from Tunas Springs southeast to the approximate location of the W. H. Mansfield home; then turning to the southwest, we ran the line across the Big Canyon to a portion of the Downie Ranch. [The head spring of Tunas Springs is 20 miles east of Fort Stockton. The W. H. Mansfield 12 section ranch was located 43 miles northeast of Sanderson in 1895. Charley Downie's large spread had its headquarters some 12 miles northwest of Sanderson.]

This was desolate, dry country, but we found a few temporary water holes and managed to get by without serious trouble. That morning, on the head arroyos of the Main Independence Draw we killed a yearling TX heifer, and loaded it into our wagon. [The headquarters of the large TX cattle spread was located near Horsehead Crossing on the Pecos.] We chained rapidly that day over a lot of country and that night we camped about 15 miles from the spot where the heifer was killed. At the end of the work day the chainmen stuck all the chaining pins in the ground at the end of the chain. Our camp was about 30 feet from the place where the pins were left.

The next morning, ready to resume work on the survey, the pins could not be found. We looked to the chainmen for an answer, and they were quite positive of the place and position in which they were left the evening before. But not a one was to be found. We were very puzzled over their disappearance. We finally located one about fifty yards from its location of the night before. Further search brought in all but two. We found that the red flannel rag which was tied to the ring of every pin was missing from every ring. This caused much speculation, but the explanation offered by our Mexican driver was finally accepted as the most probably correct — that is, that the coyotes had torn off the flannel rags and eaten them.

This was probably true, so the coyotes must have trailed us 15 miles from the carcass of the heifer. The meat being carried in the wagon left no scent, but the chainmen had handled the bloody meat, and afterwards handled the iron pins and flannel rags. The coyotes had followed the scent left on the grass across which the [chain] pins and flannel rags were drug. Possibly, if the iron pins had been manageable in the coyote's mouths, they might have been eaten also. This demonstrated not only the power of scent in the animal, but also a digestive system almost equal to that of the burro, which is reputed to occasionally make a repast of tin cans.

The animal is rare which does not have some use beneficial to the economy of man. The coyote has more than one use and probably benefits mankind in a circuitous route. Indirectly, the coyote probably renders service that is disguised or hidden amid so many intricate and unknown paths that they are not recognized. Occasionally an unexpected benefit results.

In 1880, I was in a mining camp known as Shakespeare, located in the most arid portion of Southwestern New Mexico. The camp lay in a small arroyo and depended upon two shallow wells for water. There were many other small arroyos running out of these low mountains, but no water was found in any of them. Indeed, that entire country seemed to be devoid of water. I asked how they had been able to locate that single spot of water, and was told this story: One of the men who discovered the mine was sorely troubled for water and noted the presence of coyotes. He knew that they depended upon a daily source of water, therefore, he reasoned that accessible water was somewhere in that vicinity. He set to watching the animals, and this led to the discovery of a hole about five feet deep with water at the bottom.

Camillo Terrasas [formerly an outstanding cowboy in Pecos County] tells me that about 20 years ago [1888], he and some other Mexicans chased a coyote into its hole around the division line between the Livingston and Gibson ranches in Pecos County, about 25 miles northeast of Fort Stockton. While digging it out, they discovered that the hole led to water, then took an upward course, at an angle, to the den where the coyote was found. Such incidents show that at times the animal's scent might be useful to man.

Before the arrival of man, this animal already had a wide range of eatables. "Nihil a me alienum puto!" Nothing in the animal kingdom, dead or alive, repulses it. The Mexicans say that he also levies his toll on insects, especially the grasshoppers. In this country, his main source of food must have been rabbits, jackrabbits, prairie dogs and quail. When man invaded the scene the coyote added sheep, pigs, and poultry to his bill of fare. Perhaps when they are desperately hungry they will attack a calf, although cattlemen tell me they suffer only minor losses of calves to the coyote. This fact points out the cowardice of the animal.

I have often observed that cows with young calves always leave one cow with the calves while the others go to water. This arrangement always puzzled me. I am told that Brahma cows stay with their young calves for the first few days until the calves can walk to water with them. Even with that protection, I had a few calves show up with ears split by what I assume were the teeth of a coyote.

Judge Williams' article of 1908 continues:

> The sheep, the most timid of domestic animals, is a prime favorite with the coyote. About 16 to 18 years ago a sheepherder drove his flocks along the Pecos River during a great drouth. It was doubtful that the ewes could find sustenance for themselves, much less for their lambs. The sheepman decided to kill the lambs in order to save the lives of as many mother ewes as possible.
>
> I procured some of the lambs and raised them with cow's milk, keeping them at my ranch and farm across the river opposite Grandfalls. At six or eight months old they were allowed to graze on alfalfa near the house. I kept them in an enclosed pen at night in order to protect them from coyotes and wildcats. They never went more than 500 yards from the house. One evening they deviated from their usual habit and didn't appear at sunset, so I sent a Mexican after them. He returned with all but two which he informed me had been killed by coyotes. He had tracked them on their usual evening route home where they crossed a ditch; here, the tracks turned sharply away from the house and were followed by coyote tracks. After following the trail a short distance, he found the dead body of a sheep, and then another. Further on, he found the remainder huddled together, where they had evidently been driven by four or five coyotes. Since the varmints had not stopped to eat the sheep they had killed, but had continued to drive the entire flock further from safety, it would appear that they planned to carry the flock away and devour them at their leisure.

Frequently, young pigs are their victims. In former years hogs were often allowed to graze loose on the Pecos River, where an abundance of mesquite beans and edible root called "chufas" seemed to promise a favorable opportunity for rapid increase. [Formal name for "chufas" is *cyperus esculentus,* a form of sedge.]

Yet the hogs did not increase, and it would appear this was solely due to the ravages of coyotes and wildcats on the little ones. On one occasion I saw an old sow with five little pigs trotting through an alfalfa field. Three coyotes leisurely trotted after her, and it was plain that she was headed for the safety of the house. I saw the foremost coyote make a sudden rush, seize the hindmost pig and dash away for the brush. Roused by the cries of the stolen pig, the sow turned and charged the remaining coyotes. Her pigs, of course, attempted to follow her. A coyote caught another pig and as the sow attempted to follow to rescue it, the last coyote caught a pig and ran away with it. On another occasion I had a sow sleeping within ten yards of my house with her litter of small pigs. A coyote furtively slunk up in the night grabbed a pig, and ran away with it.

Poultry is the coyote's gourmet delight. If the varmint ever once tastes the rancher's chickens, he must be killed, or the chickens will all disappear. He will persistently loiter around the vicinity, until the fowls are exhausted, or he dies. On isolated ranches, eggs and young chickens help ease the hard ranch fare, and the coyote is the bane of the good housewife's existence. Mesquite or other brush usually grow close to the house, and the wily coyote lurks in this brush, seeking to capture a succulent chicken that has strayed away from the house. With a sudden rush, the animal snatches his prey and rapidly departs to enjoy a square meal.

Unless a dog pack is relatively large, even that does not discourage the coyote. Often while the dogs are chasing one animal, another darts in and catches its prey. There may be no design in this, but it happens so often that it is apparent the coyote realizes the value and protection of numbers in hunting.

There is one habit of the coyote which I believe is worthy of mention. It will not chase or attack larger game, but it does leisurely and persistently follow larger animals. The purpose of this trailing is not obvious.

Late one afternoon in Arizona, in 1886, I was compelled to walk alone through a mountainous and uninhabited country. I thought I was being deliberately followed by two wolves for about four miles. They behaved as a dog will when trailing behind his master, only they kept their distance. Being trailed like this created some uneasiness on my part, until I finally deduced that they were coyotes.

In the summer of 1878, I was traveling horseback on the staked plains in Swisher County, Texas, and I was followed in this manner by a solitary coyote for an entire day. It required a rifle shot to end the leisurely pursuit.

Another time I encountered a lone buffalo calf being followed in this manner by several coyotes. The calf was five or six months old, ambling over the plains, manifesting no uneasiness, while the coyotes were slowly following without exhibiting any intent of immediate attack. In this case we can assume that as soon as the coyotes were reinforced by a sufficient number of comrades, an attack would be launched, unless the calf should join a herd of buffalo.

This trailing by the coyote is often done so unobtrusively and under such favorable conditions, it escapes observation, unless unexpected circumstances reveal it. Men and animals may thus be followed without becoming aware of it, unless something behind them attracts their attention.

John Summerfield and O. W. Williams had been given instructions from the General Land Office to make connections between the surveys in Blanco Canyon and those made a year before in Hale County. During that survey in 1879

Summerfield and Judge Williams killed a buffalo on the great plains. Concerning that incident, Williams wrote:

> The wagons arrived, and the men set to work butchering and loading the meat. One of the men called attention to a circle of coyotes around us. We counted eleven of them, each sitting on its haunches about 100 yards away, each to itself, quiet and watchful, apparently not in the least excited. Since nobody had seen any coyotes that morning, perhaps they were following the buffalos in the manner to which I have called attention. When the herd ran away they stayed to partake of the remains of the slain animals. They probably thus appeared on the scene of every "stand" secured by a hunter, but were unnoticed up to that point.
>
> I am told that sheepherders notice this same trait, and claim that a coyote will follow a herd for days. I do not know about the validity of this claim, but it coincides with the incident which I have already related, and is probably done for the same purpose, as sheep often stray from their herd and become a prey to the coyotes.
>
> Up to 1908, little has been done in this country to kill coyotes except those measures taken by sheepmen, who wage continual war on the animal. I am of the opinion that the coyote is just about as abundant in Pecos County today as it was 20 years ago. While the battle against it in some neighborhoods has caused it to decrease there, its comparative immunity from harm has caused it to increase in others. The northern and western parts of the county are cattle raising localities, and no war has been waged on it there. The extreme southern part is devoted more to sheep raising than to cattle, hence, in this area, the coyote has been poisoned and trapped. Perhaps each year, the southern end receives a contribution of coyotes which were raised in the northern and eastern parts. In this manner, a pretty general uniformity in number is sustained. About 1891 to 1892, a small bounty was offered by the county for coyote scalps. This bounty

was not offered long enough to determine precisely how much it would decrease the numbers of coyotes. Yet it remained in effect long enough to give rise to a very strong suspicion among the cattlemen — the decrease of the coyote meant the increase of the jackrabbit. That, in turn, meant that cattle might have less grass to eat. During those seasons when grass is abundant, this would probably matter little, but when the grass is short, it could mean a loss of cattle.

About the time this bounty was offered by the county on the scalps of coyotes there was general agitation in Western Texas, in favor of bounties and other means of ridding the frontier of animal pests. I remember one serious contention urged upon the people of West Texas as a means of ridding them of the coyote; that was — turn loose coyotes infected with mange in this county. They would communicate the scourge to others until our section would be entirely free of them. This scheme looked very plausible on paper. Many valuable experiments have been made on somewhat similar lines.

However, mange to the Pecos County coyotes may be like the poor of mankind — always with them. I have heard of mangy coyotes for at least 20 years, yet the disease has not reduced the numbers of the animal by any appreciable figure. In spite of the presence of mange, coyotes are thriving in this area. Upon closer examination, this idea appears to be worthless.

I am inclined to doubt the wisdom of suddenly eradicating any native wild animal. I am disposed to think the wisest and most conservative method of disposing of noxious wild animals would be to do so proportionately — as other contemporary animals and insects disappear, i.e., pari pasu. Even a small disturbance of nature's balance may lead to disastrous results. To illustrate: Suppose the coyote feeds upon some animal or bird, that in turn eats an animal which feeds upon grasshoppers and locusts. The chain may be a long one, and by completely destroying the coyote man might ultimately do more damage than good. This might allow grasshoppers and locusts to multiply to an extraordinary extent. A plague of grasshoppers and locusts would be far more damaging to man than the coyote.

Along with the buzzard, the coyote is classed as a carrion eater, and like that bird probably depends upon scent to find dead animals. The Mexicans say it is especially partial to a dead horse. There is no carrion it rejects, and this trait makes it an easy victim to poison. Very little attempt is made in this county to destroy the animal, except by sheep owners, upon whose flocks it inflicts considerable damage. Their common practice is to put out "baits," around a dead carcass after the animals have begun to feed upon it.

If you simply place a piece of fresh meat out with poison on top of it, the wily, cunning coyote will detect it and won't touch it. A bait is contrived by concealing strychnine in the middle of small pieces of fresh meat. The animal bolts its food and never tastes the poison. The coyote won't touch food as long as there is even a semblance of danger, but it will swallow it in an instant when there is nothing suspicious or dangerous around it.

Evidently they have some method of communication to call their brothers to a feast of carrion, yet they seem unable to profit by the experience of those which are poisoned in their presence. I once poisoned 14 of the animals in one night around the carcass of an old horse. A canal with water was close to the carrion, and I suppose they slaked their thirst after eating. Drinking water speeds the action of poison, thus they died immediately and lay close together. Otherwise they might have traveled away and died at distant points.

The effect of this poison must have been witnessed that night by some animals that were subsequently poisoned on the same night, and by others that escaped. Yet, the following night the remaining crew returned to the feast, and I secured five more. They continued returning until the carrion was entirely eaten up.

As a small girl on the Williams' farm and ranch in the 1890s, Ermine Williams Garnett, the Judge's daughter, observed the problems presented by coyotes. She recorded her experiences:

> At, or shortly before sundown, all chickens had to be fastened in the chicken house. Even so, our rate of loss was high, thanks to skunks, foxes, raccoons and coyotes roaming about the area. It was not unusual for a coyote to dart quickly into our flock of chickens while they were being fed in the early morning. The scroungy beast would seize a chicken and be off and away before we could stop him. Hawks and owls also took a heavy toll of our poultry.
> Although bobcats, skunks, pumas and raccoons all damaged our farm and ranch operations, I believe we had more trouble with coyotes than any other wild animal. If one visited a neighboring ranch without a gun, he would almost invariably see a coyote. The brazen animal would come out in plain sight, and sometimes travel parallel to the road. Sometimes they would just stop and watch you with no apparent fear or concern. When we did not hang our harness sufficiently high, or left it on the ground overnight, almost inevitably a coyote would proceed to chew it to shreds during the night.
> Our garden was tightly fenced to keep rabbits and small animals out. We had even built an old-fashioned stile over the fence, instead of making a gate for entry. Still, the coyotes raided it and destroyed large numbers of cantaloupe and watermelon just before they were ready to be picked.
> When we put out poisoned baits to kill the varmints, the dogs were tied up, and the coyotes seemed to be aware of that fact. They became increasingly bold. They would stroll into the yard in broad daylight and snatch a chicken, peacefully pecking its grain. We began to keep a loaded gun handy on a rack close to the back door, but it always seemed to be just out of reach when one of the varmints showed up.
> Our old red NA cow [from the NA cow outfit] had

a red and white spotted calf which our little sister Kathryn claimed for herself. One day we children left the gate open while we were in the calf pen. The calf escaped and ran into the tall mesquite brush close by. My brother and I followed quickly, but before we could reach him, we heard his stricken bawl, then encountered him racing directly back toward his pen, bleeding badly from a missing tail. We penned and doctored the mutilated calf, so he recovered completely — except for his missing tail — but we were never able to determine exactly what happened to him. We found large bobcat tracks in the vicinity where he had run away, but nothing else. From that time forward, he was known as "Tailless."

In writing about his irrigated garden and coyote problem on the Pecos River ranch, Williams stated:

My prized melon patch proved to be a sore temptation to the entire animal population in my neck of the woods. Coyotes, in particular, were inflicting great damage in it. Though he rejected no carrion, no matter how foul — Mr. Coyote was particular about his melons. [Perhaps they were his dessert!] He haughtily refused all but ripe melons — and he could infallibly detect the ripe ones. He liked them all, put preferred cantaloupes. I brought the bane of the coyote to my aid — strychnine.

The tracks of the animal indicated that they came over my garden fence at the same spot every night. I placed a ripe cantaloupe or two, with poison concealed inside them, at this spot, outside the garden fence. I picked the smallest ones I could find, so that perhaps the animals would bolt them whole. This plan proved successful, and coyotes were thus poisoned, night after night, until the last of the varmints aware of my preserves "turned up its toes."

The coyote makes its home — if an animal which roams so constantly can have a home — in the plains and flats. Rock caves are plentiful in this county, but rather than use them, the coyote will dig a hole in the ground. The young coyotes are littered in this hole, and they will rarely be seen out of it by day, until they are more than three-fourths grown. When six or seven coyotes are seen together in the daytime, it may be safely assumed that they consist of an old female and her pups.

In order to remain on the subject of coyote dens we leave Judge Williams' narrative to listen to the old government trapper, Charlie Stone, as he tells us about that subject:

Coyotes usually build their dens in canyons or under rock ledges. Sometimes they build their dens in an old badger hole or they will dig out a rat mound. Possibly they'll build in an arroyo bed or a wash under a cliff. We use a pick and shovel to dig them out. Sometimes they go four, five or six feet deep. Then they go back ten or fifteen feet. Then they have two or three little pockets the pups go back into.

The pups are born about April or May. The mother will suckle them for two or three weeks. When they get large enough she will catch food, predigest it and then vomit it up for the pups to eat. At this time, she will not let them nurse anymore. Sometimes an old male coyote will have a couple of females with puppies and he will help feed the little ones. These two females will live in the same den with two bunches of puppies, altogether, twelve or fourteen little ones. I have found this to happen a number of times when coyotes were more plentiful than now. I have found them in dens where the old coyotes were killing small calves and bringing the fresh meat to the den to feed the pups.

These old wolves are very cautious about their puppies. When there is any danger around the old coyote will usually bark and run by the den and all little coyotes will scat to the den and stay in that den until mamma calls them out when the danger is over.

I have hid in the hills for hours at a time waiting to get a shot at the old coyotes. I always liked a noisy old hound when I was hiding near the den. The more noise the dog made was the better. Usually the old coyote will charge the dog and naturally the dog will come back to me. Then I can kill the old coyote, because it is after the dog which will bring him close where I can shoot him from my hiding place.

You are then ready for some hard pick-and-shovel work in digging out the pups. I have found as many as three dens in a day's time, and that is another story to keep those puppies in the den until you have time to work after them. If you have a den and do not stop it up tight as a cement block the pups will dig out and the old coyote will move to parts unknown and you have to hunt for them again. The parents stay with the pups for five or six months, then the pups get out of control and root for themselves.

You know at times a rattlesnake will be in the same den with the coyotes. In one instance Pat Foster and I found one on the ranch of the late Hood Mendel in Pecos County. This den was located under a big rat's nest. While Pat was digging down the earth gave way into another hole. Pat said that although some earth followed his foot into the cavity below, he felt that his foot was resting upon a snake. Quickly he pulled out his foot and climbed out. Along with him came two coyote-puppies and a rattlesnake. As soon as the snake got out, it took a look at Pat, raised its tail and started at him — "The funniest thing," Pat said, "I ever saw."

Charlie didn't think it was funny when the snake raised its tail and charged Pat — he thought that was the wrong use of the word *funny*. He shot the reptile before it could reach Pat — but Pat was not at all certain the snake hadn't made contact with him on the way out of the hole. He undressed and inspected his body to see if there were any signs of snakebite. This was what Charley found hilarious. I'll let the old trapper continue his tale:

But it was funny to see Foster shed all his clothes

in search of a possible snake bite when anybody should know if and where he had been snake bit.

One day we were digging a den this side of Pecos. If there was one flea in that den there was a million. They covered us up. We killed the pups. Other animals don't den in the same hole because the wolf will kill them.

One time in 1933 near Girvin, Texas, there was a coyote killing Cunnningham sheep. His ranch hands had been chasing and making drives to destroy it for a year. Mr. Landom [in charge of predatory animal control], Mr. Hill and Eddie Ligon and myself went down there and spent the night. The next morning they brought in the horses for us to ride on the coyote drive. They didn't have any horses worth anything. I got stuck with a three-legged horse.

The rest of them spread out across the pasture to ride across it to look for the coyote, but I went along the fence line for a couple of miles. They didn't have any airplanes. It was all on horseback. After the coyote was jumped on the east side of the pasture, they were chasing and shooting at him when I cut across the pasture and ran right into that wolf. I shot and killed him deader'n Hell with the first shot out of my pistol. Cunningham said, "By golly, we've been chasing that coyote a year and we've shot a trainload of cartridges and never have hit him. I'm glad we got him because if we hadn't, it would have put a bad reputation on the government hunters." That coyote had killed about two or three hundred sheep before we got him.

Destruction of coyotes has been modernized since Judge Williams poisoned carcasses with strychnine and let the coyotes gorge themselves. The professional trapper of twenty years later often caught animals in his traps he was not at all anxious to have, such as skunks, rabbits and other varmints. The trapper would drag a quarter of beef around the region where his traps were set, poison it and leave it lying in order to get rid of the so-called "trash" before it reached his traps.

The steel traps were then entrenched in holes in likely places. The trapper stood upon the springs, mashed down to hold open the jaws of the trap, set the trigger, and the deadly contrivance waited for some unfortunate animal to step upon it. The trapper gave due credence to the intelligence of a trap-wise coyote, which had either experienced the effect of a trap, or had seen one of his brothers caught in one. The trap was covered with a light piece of canvas and all of it was overlaid with a shallow coating of dirt in order to leave the impression that there was no trap. Some kind of bait was added to this, preferably the urine of some member of the dog family — as they are all in the habit of smelling each other's calling card.

Charley Stone said: "I bait my traps with scent. Wolf urine is what I usually use for coyotes. In order to get this scent for bait, you take this pet coyote and put him in a box with a steel bottom with a slope. A trough is put in one end and a bucket at the bottom of the slope. In this manner the coyote's urine is caught in the bucket. We catch a pup coyote and he gets gentle. And he'll give you all the bait you want. We do the same way with a bobcat."

With his family, twelve-year-old Lloyd Ligon traveled from San Angelo to Pecos County in 1901. They crossed the Pecos River at Lancaster Crossing — then known as Flat Rock Crossing. It had formerly been the Overland Stage Crossing where the river spread out with an island located in the middle. This site is about one and one-half miles below the present State Highway 290 bridge on the river. The ferry across the Pecos was then operating about two miles up river from Lancaster Crossing.

The Ligons settled on a farm, on the Pecos, in Reeves County and were among the first water well drillers in Pecos County. The boys were diligent workers, covering all of Pecos County and some other counties in their work and eventually became the owners and operators of their own ranches. In his elder years, Lloyd Ligon had his wife, Nora, write the following story for me:

In 1926 I had 600 ewes in a six section pasture. In December the ewes started lambing, and while they were lambing I found 50 baby lambs that had been killed by coyotes. A baby lamb will run to anything that moves, and they are easy prey for a coyote. The coyotes had killed them by biting them in the back of the head, and they had eaten the livers and drank the milk out of the lamb's stomachs.

Before and while I was lambing, I caught and killed about 25 coyotes, but there was one female that I couldn't catch in a trap. I had set traps for her all winter. Several times I found her tracks in the snow and in the dust where she had come close to the traps and jumped over them, clearing them by several feet.

I offered a one hundred dollar reward to anyone who could catch this coyote, but nobody else tried to catch her. It looked as if my only chance to get her was to chase her with dogs.

A three-legged dog coyote came in to the little female. Every morning for several weeks, Theodore Lewis, a man who was working for me, chased these coyotes with my dogs, one of them a bloodhound. The dogs would get on the trail of the dog coyote, and the little female would trail along behind Theodore and the dogs and bark at them. Finally Theodore chased the dog coyote out of the pasture, but he soon came back to the female.

I set a trap in the hole where the coyote had been going under the new wire fence. The trap was placed in a dug place, its jaws were set and covered with a canvas and dirt in order to hide its existence. The dog coyote was caught by its upper jaw. The coyote was minus one front foot, having been caught before in a trap and had made his escape then by leaving that foot in the trap. In this last encounter with a trap, he had recognized the site of the trap and had dug around its outside in order to clear it of dirt. But in the effort to lift it out with his mouth, being afraid to place his foot there, his upper jaw had been caught.

One day a government trapper who was working for Jim Rooney brought his two hounds over, and with my two dogs we went on a drive to get the female coyote. We chased her nearly all morning. We knew the dogs were on her trail, but she evaded them by running across the pasture in a figure eight, over and over. When she came to the fence she doubled back in a figure eight again. All the dogs except the bloodhound — Big Boy, I called him — jumped fence, but Big Boy turned back on her trail. The other dogs circled about a hundred yards, then came back and took up the trail again with Big Boy.

After a long chase all the dogs, except Big Boy, got hot and tired and quit running, so we stopped to rest awhile, but I had to make Big Boy rest. He wanted to go after that coyote. I told the trapper that this was one time I was going to stay with Big Boy as long as he wanted to chase that coyote.

About that time we saw the coyote trotting away from us. I told the trapper to follow the dogs after the coyote and I would take a stand on a hill in a bunch of cedar bushes out of sight along the figure eight path that the coyote had been running all morning. I tied my horse down in the creek out of sight and ran up on the hill to wait. Finally I heard the dogs barking, and in a little while the coyote ran close by me. I shot her in the head and killed her instantly. When she fell Big Boy chewed her up a little, but he wouldn't let any of the other dogs come near her.

A coyote might make a fool of a man, but not that bloodhound, Big Boy!

Ligon told me of another instance when the coyote made a "monkey" of man. The coyote cleverly extracted the dirt and canvas covering off the top of the trap, carried it a short distance away and deposited his excretion on top of it to signify his utter contempt for man and his science of trapping.

The late Montie Wallace reported the following:

> Mr. Lanham sent me to the Devil's River area because there was a coyote killing buck deer. This was

the toughest country to trap in because it was so rocky. The coyote was not digging under the net wire fence because it was so tightly wired, but either jumping or crawling over it. When I had been there four or five days, I found out where it was working. After I picked out my place to put my traps, I couldn't find enough dirt at hand to hide them. I had to go down to the bottom of the hill to find that small amount of dirt. The trap had a good hook and chain.

That very night I caught the coyote. Somehow he got over that fence with the trap on his foot without getting hung up. The next day I got my dog, put him over the fence and he got on the trail of the coyote and found it about two hundred yards away. That was the first time that I ever experienced a coyote getting over a wire fence with a trap. I've had several coyotes try to go over but they never made it. I've baited some freshly killed rabbits with government poison and killed two coyotes and two eagles with them. There was a coyote going into the Pyle Country of Pecos County every once in a while. I had some traps set for it. One day one of the traps was gone. I went about thirty or forty feet farther and the coyote came out of hiding. I thought it was the funniest coyote I ever saw. After I shot it I found that somebody had caught it and cut both ears off and let it loose. The coyote showed that it had been previously trapped on two legs. The spots where they had cut off the ears were black as they could be without any hair on them. I've caught thousands of bobcats. They usually kill sheep by catching the top of the neck. They feed off of the neck and the loin. A coyote will will catch the sheep by the bottom of the neck and generally eat the ham.

Charlie Stone told of another method of luring coyotes into traps:

One time old man J. E. Hill told me that he was having trouble in trying to catch a couple of old coyote dogs on the McKenzie ranch and on down to Jim Blackstones, about thirty miles east of Fort Stockton. In order to help him, I staked out my pet female coyote as a decoy. I was camped out there by myself in the vicinity of the dog coyotes. One morning Mr. Hill came down to my camp and said, "Let's take a run down there on horseback and maybe we'll jump those old wolves."

A big wind was coming in from the west. We had gotten within a quarter mile of that female, and were riding down a canyon when Mr. Hill jumped those two coyotes. He raced behind the animals on to the top of the hill. There, he shot one through the mouth, knocked all of the teeth out of its lower jaw. The other one got clean away.

I told Hill I was going to see about my pet coyote, give it water to drink and feed it. The pet was tied to a big old stake in the ground with a big chain on it. I had placed a barrel with the top cut out for her to sleep in. When I got there I found that she had got wrapped up in the chain.

As I pulled on the chain she jumped and bit me on the face. I've got a scar right between my eyes. Boy there was blood all over the place — on my shirt and on my face. I almost killed her right there but I decided she was just protecting herself.

One time I was running a trap line on John Bennett's ranch, twelve miles north of Fort Stockton. I saw a man rounding up goats. I stopped and talked to him a while. While he was rounding up those goats, he jumped this coyote out and it ran under the fence by the road. There it was caught by a trap. The coyote then ran on down that fence and I got out of my pickup and started chasing him on foot. He turned and charged right down that road at me. I didn't have my gun or a club or nothing and was fifty yards from my pickup. As the animal arrived I tried to kick him but I lost my footing and fell down. By that time the coyote had hold of my pants, down by my boot. I sure was lucky he didn't have my leg. Pretty soon I broke loose, got me a rock and I sure took after that coyote. Boy it was in pain and mad 'cause it was in that trap.

Once I trapped a wolf coyote and I got my gun and got out of the pickup. The hook of the trap was already caught on a bush. I got too close and it made a lunge for me, and caught my leg above the knee and clamped hard. I still have two fang marks where he bit me. I reached in my pocket, got my knife and stabbed him around the heart. He came loose quick.

I used a lot of cyanide guns, or coyote-getters, because they work — hot, dry, wet or cold. I put bait on this pipe and when the animal pulls it with his mouth it shoots cyanide into his mouth and it goes into his lungs and kills him.

About three years ago a man with a surveying crew near Fort Stockton pulled a cyanide gun with his hand. It shot into his flesh, went into his bloodstream. They took him in to see a doctor but he died anyway. Cyanide guns are outlawed now. You can't buy any kind of animal poison or the cyanide gun.

When asked about the speed of a coyote, Charlie said, "I've run coyotes in a car to find out how fast they are. I've run 'em up to fifty miles per hour for a mile. I run up behind them and put my gun out the window. The riding is pretty rough but not too bad in the flat country.

"A lot of times a group of coyotes will chase a jackrabbit. First one coyote will chase the rabbit right in front of another coyote and it will catch it or if it doesn't they'll do it again or have another coyote waiting to take up the chase."

Charlie's coyotes ran a little faster than the one which got in my car lights at night while I was driving at a speed of forty miles per hour. I stayed right behind it, for it appeared to be fearful of leaving the lights of the car and racing out of the road into the dark unknown. After following right on its tail at that speed for about two miles, I increased my speed to forty-five miles per hour and ran over it.

Charlie said, "Back in 1937, one time on old man Camp's ranch near Pecos, they called Mr. Hill. He sent me and Eddie Ligon up there because the coyotes were rabid [had rabies], and were biting the cattle. They had already killed three cows that got the hydrophobia. It was in April and I went up there and the coyotes were as thick as fiddles in Georgia. I killed a lot of coyotes. There were seven cows that got hydrophobia and they had to kill all of them.

"I saw one cow come to a water trough just a-bawling, swinging her head, slobbering, her eyes back in her head and staggering. They didn't charge because they go blind. We killed a lot of coyotes and the hydrophobia stopped."

My old friend, Tom Moore, formerly of Fort Stockton and now a resident of Fort Davis, related some of his experiences while chasing coyotes with hounds.

> I used two different kinds of dogs to trail and kill coyotes: the Walker and the Trigg. I never used bloodhounds because my kind of hounds were long-winded and could run longer than the bloodhound. I had two good dogs for coyotes. Ernest Riggs [of Fort Stockton] and I ran those. Ernest had some good Trigg dogs and I had a good white dog and a red speckled one I liked best.
>
> Well, sometimes we'd run a coyote for four or five hours and cover an area of forty miles before the dogs got them down. And they didn't always get them down. As a rule coyotes run in circles. We'd run them in that sandy country of Monahans and Penwell. As a rule we hardly ever left camp. We just let our dogs loose and hear them running in circles after the coyote.
>
> When the dogs got through running it and we got there, the coyote was generally stiff and dead-run itself to death. The reason the dogs caught it was some dogs were after it all the time. Some dogs would rest while the others were hot on the trail and chasing the coyote.
>
> After a rain was the best time to trail and chase coyotes in damp weather and high grass. When the

coyote goes through wet or damp grass the scent stays on the grass. In dry or barren spots the scent doesn't stick. The dogs don't lose the trail unless they run into such dry or barren spots or when the coyote takes off straight out and away from the region we are hunting in.

Two or three times I have had experience with what I thought was a coyote with rabies. I've run them with dogs. When the dogs could catch up with it, the coyote would back up into a bush, snap and slobber but the dogs wouldn't go near it. In the second stage of hydrophobia they snap at anything: a bush or anything that gets in their way.

We return to Charlie Stone: "You can have an idea how old a coyote is by looking at whether his teeth are worn out or by the condition of the hair on the head — you can figure out whether it is an old coyote or not. When you run a coyote through greasewood and 'osane' brush [Hojasen, Tarbush or Blackbush-Flourensic cernus], your dogs lose the trail because they can't smell anything else in that stuff. Sometimes when you run a coyote with dogs another coyote might cross the trail and the dogs split up. A coyote likes to eat up the insides of a sheep and the heart and the brisket. When the cactus is in fruit the coyote will eat the petaya and the prickly pear."

I have a saying relative to one's muscles or property — use it or lose it. In respect to property, one loses its benefits if it is not used, while unused muscles become flacid. Judge Williams wrote a scientist's viewpoint concerning the coyote's use of its tail:

> Many years ago I was driving near Santa Rosa Spring with a gentleman of some scientific pretensions. He called my attention to two coyotes racing off through the brush, neither of which had a tail, and remarked that he had seen one the day before in the same mutilated condition. On this premise he proceeded to build up quite a theory, which ran thusly: That

the tail was a member absolutely useless to the wolf, and therefore destined to become an organ termed "rudimentary" by scientists. It would probably be entirely omitted from the animal's physique. It was preserved in the dog and saved from becoming rudimentary, because the dog used it to express its sentiments; the dog testifies to its feelings at both ends — with its head and tail. Therefore, the tail is a useful and important member to that animal. With the wolf the case was different. It expressed no sentiment, or meaning, by, or through its tail. In fact it could not curl its tail over its back like a dog, but was compelled to carry it as Little Bo-Peep's sheep carried theirs — behind. The tail served no beneficial purpose to the animal.

He concluded that Mother Nature's disposition to curtail the wolf's use of his tail meant that any little incident or accident might tend to rush the tailless evolution of the animal; that Dr. Brown-Sequard's recent experiments in breeding rats whose tails had been cut off finally brought around a sort of hereditary tendency in that strain of rats to be born without tails. There were evidently three tailless coyotes around Santa Rosa, which showed a tendency on the part of coyotes in that neighborhood to be born without tails; and that this hereditary tendency might become so great in a few years that a great number of tailless coyotes might be found in that locality.

The Lobo
(A Large Member of the Canine or Wolf Family)

When Coronado saw his first bison (buffalo) on the plains, he also caught sight of his first gray, or lobo, wolf. The gray wolf was following the buffalo. The gray predators trailed every band of bison and lived off the young, weak, aged or straggling buffalo. Indians told of some instances when gray wolves were bold enough to enter their tepees and fight their dogs.

When the buffalo was exterminated, the plains lobo

was compelled to look for another source of food. The fleet antelope occasionally fell victim to a lobo pack. The wolves would chase the animal in relays until it was exhausted. Cattle were easy prey for wolves. It was not unusual to see a big, bobbed-tailed steer. Quite often a tail was snipped off by a lobo which grabbed for the loin and caught the tail. Lobos caught by a lariat have been known to cut a half-inch rope with one snap of their powerful jaws.

Ranchers of Pecos County were harassed by lobos in the 1890s and managed to get a bounty placed on them by county officials. This caused more rapid extermination of the lobo and gave the stockmen some relief.

In 1908, the late O. W. Williams wrote:

> In this country, we have a wolf larger than the coyote; and it is swifter, fiercer and much more destructive to domestic flocks. It is not more bloodthirsty than the panther — a single panther may inflict more damage in one night, than any solitary wolf would inflict. But the panther may be easily trailed and destroyed after his night of carnage. The cunning wolf may continue to destroy to a ripe old age. Its cunning and its persistent diabolical pursuit of its prey lead one to understand the existence of the French Canadian belief in the werewolf.
>
> Early settlers in our area were familiar with the animal, and it is still known as the gray or timber wolf in most of this country. All along the Mexican border, and in the southwest, the name "lobo" has almost entirely supplanted the old Anglo-Saxon name. I have chosen to use lobo in this article. This was the name of the Spanish wolf of the Pyrenees and the mountains of Spain. The reader who has followed Robinson Crusoe on his return through Spain will recognize the characteristic similarity between that wolf and our wolf. Recalling Crusoe's adventures with the Pyrenean wolves, we must allow for some exaggeration in Defoe's account of the Spanish wolf.

Starvation has often caused our timber wolf to pursue human beings. . . . And I am inclined to believe that if a deep mantle of snow covered our plains every winter; and our domestic animals were housed and safe — any belated traveler by night who hears the mournful, hungry howl of the lobo should make his unfortunate horse lather until he found shelter — for he might well fear attack.

Of all the European names applied to American animals by new settlers the Spanish term, *lobo,* is probably the most appropriate. The European wolf was more similar to its American namesake than any other Old World animal. We had two types of wolves here, and the Spaniards wisely named one lobo, and accepted the indigenous name of coyote for the other.

Of all predators which prey upon our herds and flocks in 1908, the lobo inflicts the most damage, and causes stockmen the most trouble. It is not that it causes any sudden, large loss, but it is a constant, steady source of loss. It is not a calamity, such as the hordes of locusts and grasshoppers which have devastated the west a few times. It is more like a grievous tax that is laid on year by year, which must be borne with patience, and is counted every year as an entry in the columns of profit and loss.

Yet these animals are not now and have never been numerous in our county. Twenty-five years ago there was said to be but one pack of lobos in Pecos County. They ranged on the Pecos River about 30 miles above Sheffield. Then, as now, they depended upon herds of cattle for sustenance. The cattle of the "S" and Mule Shoe brands were the principal prey of this pack. Cattle had been introduced into Pecos County only a short time before, and I am unable to say whether or not the lobo made its appearance here before we brought cattle. Early settlers believed that it came here after the cattle appeared. I am disposed to think, for several reasons, that this was probably the case.

As its English name "timber wolf" indicates, the wolf prefers to inhabit wooded country and forests.

Our area is a land of plains. We have no forests, trees are exceedingly rare, and coverts of small brush are infrequent. The country was even more sparse 25 years ago. There must have been good and sufficient cause to bring the wolf into the type of environment that animal normally avoids. It wouldn't be too puzzling if an abundance of food were present. Within historic times the buffalo doesn't appear to have ever been abundant in this section. The deer and antelope were not copious, and were also animals capable of escaping the wolf's pursuit.

Apparently in early times, nature did not allow for the wolf in the economy of this county. But when cattle were moved in, large herds ranged over an immense area of the unfenced country. With such huge herds and vast pastures, cattlemen could give their herds only minimal protection. The cattle were necessarily turned loose to fend for themselves. This condition was favorable to the appearance and increase of the lobo population. Though the forest and glade were absent, the mesas and the rocky caverns around the mesa furnished shelter for the lobo. The abundance of cattle and the scant protection provided by the owners gave the cunning wolf every opportunity to thrive.

Such conditions allowed the lobo to extend its range. First we began to hear of its ravages at the Tunas Spring, 22 miles east of Fort Stockton. Then we heard of it about the old Neighbors ranch, 40 miles south of Fort Stockton. Later, it became troublesome in the foothills of the Glass Mountains both on the north side and the south side. Very early, the wolf marked himself a well defined area of territory in which it is always found. Ravages outside this territory are rare and transitory.

The northern and western end of the county have remained free from lobos. These portions are fairly level, destitute of caves and good hiding places, and are without mesas or rocky hills. But the southern and southeastern parts of the county are land with high, but small table lands separated by valleys of various widths. Here, the lobo has found a congenial home and safe retreat. If a straight line were drawn on the Pecos County map from Horsehead Crossing on the Pecos River to the Glass Mountains this line would mark approximately the northern and northwestern limits of damage done by wolves. This same area is also where the most damage has been inflicted. The animal seldom appears to the north and west of this line. It is always present to the south and east.

The mesa country was opened up to cattlemen by water wells, tanks, and fenced pastures. Shortly thereafter, the lobo extended his range and multiplied, and cattlemen faced the necessity of dealing with this scourge of the great dry divide. War was declared on the lobo, and no truce has ever been called. At times, the ranchmen's battle is feeble, and at other times energetic. Several efforts have been launched in hopes of completely extirpating the animal, but lack of a common, united and unanimous attack has prevented such a wholesale undertaking from being successful. At present, every individual cattle owner tries to protect himself, and uses various methods of defense.

Each individual generally keeps dogs. The dogs chase the lobo from their master's immediate locality and no further. When the animal has been driven away, the individual is content until lobo returns or another appears — then the chase and exodus is repeated. Manifestly, this is a case of "scotching" the snake, and no more. The lobos are not destroyed, but simply kept moving from ranch to ranch. It could easily be that as one wolf is driven back and forth from ranch to ranch like a tennis ball, he could inflict as much damage during his coming and going as though he had remained undisturbed.

This course of action is explained by two facts: First, the comparative ease with which a lobo is temporarily driven off any particular range by persistent chasing with dogs; and second, the great difficulty and lack of success in more radical measures attempting the destruction of the animal. The lobo is not only a very swift animal; it is also exceedingly wary, probably more so than any other wild animal found in these parts. The fox hound is too slow and suffers too much from heat and tender feet to be successful in chasing it in this country. The greyhound suffers a similar fate, and in addition, cannot cope with the wolf if he is overtaken. The horseman mounted on the swiftest horse fares even worse than the greyhound on the mesas and hills, the lobo's favorite playgrounds.

The following tale cites one of the relatively rare occasions when a wolf chase was successful. I relate it as it was told to me: Several years ago, some cowboys on the Gibson & Baldridge ranch sited several lobos near Horsehead Crossing on the Pecos River. Immediately they gave chase. Though their mounts were not swift, they were fortunate enough to catch up with the wolves and rope three of them. This unexpected success was accounted for by three concurring circumstances. First, the chase occurred in very level country, and the lobos lost the advantage of racing over hills which the horses could not climb. Second, the animals were young and not fully grown. Last, but not least important, the wolves had recently gorged and then gone to the river and filled up with water. They were returning thus heavily laden, when the cowboys pursued and captured them.

The latter condition can rarely be induced by man, for the lobo generally drinks and feeds at night. Outlaw horses and other animals have been caught by this method — keeping them from food and water as long as possible, then letting them gorge or quench their thirst. However, any plan man devises must be adapted to the habits of the animal he is trying to trap. Evidently this method cannot be adapted to the native habits of the lobo, and it is not a successful trapping method.

According to records, other methods are equally unsuccessful. Where the greedy coyote gobbles up poisoned bait, the wary old lobo is rarely caught by that method. I have heard of only one case where bait was successful in killing a lobo. Strychnine was placed in the flesh of the shoulder of a live sheep. The sheep was staked in the path the lobo was accustomed to traveling, and the lobo was killed, after catching and eating the poisoned sheep. This is the only successful case of poisoning I have heard of, and I can only conclude that poisoning is a failure with the lobo.

At times lobos become so troublesome that considerable rewards are offered for their scalps by individuals on whose property they are raiding. Only a few years ago the sum of $50 was paid for the killing of a particular lobo which depredated on a large scale about ten miles from Fort Stockton. And $20 a head is a common price paid by ranchmen for killing lobos on their ranches. This may seem to be a high price; but I have no doubt it is worth much more than that to the ranchmen. About five years ago, I heard of a lobo which killed nine calves on nine successive days on a ranch not far from Fort Stockton. If these calves were worth only $5 each — that lobo destroyed $45 worth of property in a little over a week and during its lifetime may have inflicted hundreds of dollars worth of damage.

There are professional hunters who make a lifetime career of hunting wolves for reward money. Some of them become quite expert in the field, and others consider it only temporary employment.

Most hunters rely on various traps. The professional ability of the hunter is probably measured by the skill with which he conceals his traps. Every effective device is adopted that will remove the scent of man from the trap or bait. Some of the measures taken seem ludicrous and fanciful — certainly some of the procedures would surprise an ordinary man. I sometimes think that a man who devotes himself to this business will inevitably develop into that superstitious frame of mind which gave birth to the myth of the "man/wolf" in ancient times.

If the lobo has any useful qualities or habits I have not yet learned of them. If it destroys any noxious animal, reptile or insect in appreciable quantity, I have no account of it. It seems to be a specialist in carnage and to have brought professional skill to the slaughter of cattle. Possibly it has its uses — but it will require a skillful man with a very high powered magnifying glass to ascertain them.

The late Montie Wallace, of Fort Stockton, helped to eliminate the last of the lobos in Pecos County. Montie was reported to have been one of the best shots in the country. Henry Scruggs worked on the T. M. Pyle Ranch during the last days of the lobos, and now lives in Fort Stockton. Henry said he and Montie once spotted two eagles on the platform of a windmill. Montie shot one while it was sitting, and got the other in flight with a 30-30 Winchester rifle. Scruggs said that Wallace had a standing offer of a dollar bet that he could toss an empty .22 shell into the air and shoot it with his .22 rifle. Scruggs said nine out of ten times, Wallace won the bets.

The following interview with Montie Wallace, concerning lobos, was taped on July 10, 1972:

> We moved to the plains in 1903 or 1904, where I spent most of my time till 1916. My daddy used to trap in that canyon east of the town of Canyon (Palo Duro), and I did too after I growed up. Ever since I was big enough to carry a trap, I've trapped. I didn't use the same kind of trap on a lobo as I did on a coyote. On a lobo I used a No. 4 Newhouse, a trap almost as large as a bear trap. The two hooks on the chain attached to the trap were turned opposite and like an anchor. The hooks will catch up on grass and other shrubs and stop a coyote. But a lobo will pull these hooks loose from anything as weak as grass.
>
> A lobo has its pups in a cave and its young stay with it. A coyote's young will not. I would set a trap on top of the hook and chain, and cover it with paper, grass, and dirt until the animal couldn't see the trap. I would then put Tonquin Musk on it to give the set a sweet, but strong odor, to simulate a female in heat. I used that only for lobos. For a coyote I would use dog urine.
>
> When I was working for the government and camped at the Harris ranch southeast of Rankin in 1915, my boss, Lanham, came to my camp and told me to move to the N. H. Ranch, where a bunch of lobos was killing a calf every two or three days. The ranch

was managed by the older Childers boys. Bill Long also was working over there and had been for eight months. Lanham wanted me to go over there and help Long try to catch those lobos. I got over there about the third of September.

Long had his camp about three-quarter mile away from where those lobo pups were raised. He'd been camped there and trying to catch those lobos quite some time. He'd been working after the old ones and hadn't caught an old wolf at all before the pups were born. By then, at the time I got there, the pups were big — eight months old, and almost as big as the old ones. They were not as big as the Newfoundland dog, just bigger than a police dog.

Long said he had, at that time, set out about a hundred traps. With that many traps out, I was wondering where I was going to set my traps because I couldn't trap where his traps were. So I rode his line of traps with him to find out where not to set mine. He had caught two pups the very day I got there and another on the third day. I rode the trapline with him the next day, carrying some of my traps on my saddle. After which, I went out on his range and set two traps.

The next morning I went with him on his line again. We got off before daylight and went about two miles from camp when we found one of his traps throwed. The trap had failed to catch some animal after being sprung. Since I had a couple of traps on my saddle, I went on to the other side of his line to the east.

I was sitting on my horse while he was fooling with his traps when I saw a pack of seven pups and the old female coming around a path about five hundred yards away. I told Bill I saw them and asked him to take the traps off of his saddle so we could chase the wolves without carrying the traps. When the pack came around a point, the young wolves were following a path, and the old female had gotten up the hill about one hundred yards when she saw us. Boy! She really left there.

The pups never did see us, or see her leave, so we went right up the canyon. I hold Bill, "We've got to circle this canyon and that hill to get out of the windward side from the pups, so they can't smell us." Then we circled the hill and rode three quarters of a mile gettin' there. Bill wanted to take the lower ledge. So I said I'd take the other one and the top. Well I had a space of about fifteen or twenty feet before another bunch of brush. The hill kinda came out and went up above. So we got off our horses and were walking as close as I wanted to that ledge where I could see everything. I knew the wolves would surely come out there. I heard Bill shoot. In a minute he shot again. Then two pups came out on top and I got both of them before they got out of sight. Then two more came and I got one of them. The other one topped out around 150-200 yards up the hill and I shot him. Another one came out, but I didn't see it then because I was watching that other one.

By then, Bill had come up the hill. I looked across the canyon and saw a pup agoin' out on the other side, about two hundred yards away, goin' north. I cut down on him and knocked him down. He got up and I thought I'd shoot another bullet at him but I was out of ammunition. I hollered at Bill and he said, "I haven't got any bullets, I've shot all mine up."

So I went and got my horse, got on him and took after the pup. I ran him about six or seven hundred yards and he wouldn't get off the hill. Finally I got him off on to the flats, rode by a mesquite tree, pulled off a dead limb about four or five feet long and managed to ride up even with the pup and knocked him down. Then I got off my horse and clubbed the young lobo to death.

As my horse was afraid of the wolf, I had to tie one of the horse's front feet up under his belly in order to get the wolf on his back. When I got to the top, Bill had brought all six dead wolves together. The one I brought made seven pups. Bill had killed two and I had killed five.

That evening we went back and tried to call that old she-wolf up. We used our hands and tried to sound like a pup. And I couldn't even hear from her.

I went back the next day and run my traps that

I had set. In one of them I found the old male wolf. Following that, I went back to Harris', leaving Bill with that female to catch. He stayed there two months and couldn't do nothing with her. I trapped a male lobo at Harris'.

Lanham got another man in January. He set out a line. That very night it snowed about four inches. He couldn't see his line as the traps were covered and could have been gone and he wouldn't know it. A wolf got caught the night he put out his traps, before it snowed, and he never did find it. So he sent for and got Childers Long to help. Lanham sent him in to Pecos. As he was riding across the N. H. Ranch he saw where a trap was being dragged. He sent and caught Bill and told him to go get the wolf because the tracks were fresh. Bill got on his horse, went down there, the dogs picked up the trail, went half a mile and caught up with the she-wolf. That was the wolf that got away with the trap just ahead of the snow. In the fury of the fight the wolf broke out of the trap. But as it was weak from dragging the trap the dogs caught and killed it. That was the end of the wolves east of the Pecos in Upton, Reagan and Crockett counties.

I have caught lots of lobos west of the Pecos. At that time, there were more lobos west of the Pecos than there were near to and east of the Pecos.

A pack of lobos would usually kill a calf every two or three days. A lobo would jump up and grab and hold a big chunk of the loin of a calf and pull it down. Then the pack would kill and eat it.

I didn't move into the T. M. Pyle country in southern Pecos County until 1919, immediately after World War I. For some time, Mr. Pyle wanted me to catch a lobo and bring it to him alive so he could send it to San Antonio. In 1921, I'd set some traps out on the P Bar outfit and I saw where one of them had caught a wolf up there. I thought I might take this wolf alive for Mr. Pyle. I went and got my dog and trailed it about a mile and a half. Those P Bar hills, just north of the P Bar, were real high. The wolf got just about halfway up the hill with the trap on its leg. In order to try to capture the wolf alive I went and got a big old rope I had. But it wasn't a lariat. It was just a three-quarter-inch rope. I thought I would try to take the wolf because he wasn't hung up. In following the animal with the trap on its foot, the dog ran him off the hill and into the brush in a canyon.

I figured he would have to hang up the hooks on the chains attached to the trap on some brush limbs, or I couldn't catch him. I got off of my horse and went into the brush to see if he had hung up. Suddenly I was at him. He charged me. I couldn't run uphill far because of the steepness of the hill. Luckily my dog caught up with me and attracted the lobo's attention before he got to me. Then I attempted to rope him. He charged me again and the dog again saved me. As he hadn't got caught in the brush and I couldn't get close enough to rope him, I went to my horse, took the gun from my saddle and killed him. So ended that attempt to take a live lobo to Mr. Pyle.

The last lobo in T. M. Pyle country was a white one. I had heard of it for five years. A. M. Cone said he would pay five hundred dollars to anybody who would kill the white lobo. That was a lot of money in those days. I trapped and trapped. I could never understand why I had not succeeded in catching the white wolf.

One day I was on my way to T. M. Pyle country. Because it had rained I figured it would be easier to travel on the Round Mountain rather than the Sanderson road. I had just passed the Round Mountain hill when the white lobo crossed the road just ahead of me. I traveled at least twenty-five steps before it saw me. I figured then that it couldn't hear or it would have heard me as I traveled noisily along. It then was startled and ran fifty yards and stopped and looked back. I was almost certain that there were more wolves in that vicinity, but I didn't have my gun and I couldn't do anything about it. I was almost certain that the wolf couldn't hear or it would not have let me get that close to it when my horse was jogging along the road. That was a year before I finally killed it. In 1925 I went back to the T. M. Pyle country working for Downie, who sent me word that there was a lobo in the Pyle country. Ed Downie had a doctor visiting him from San Antonio who wanted to go deer hunting. One morning the doctor wanted to go with me on the wolf hunt and I agreed to take him. I knew the wolf was killing and staying in the Clarot country. If I could frighten it out of hiding, I might be able to kill it. We rode to the Clarot hill in the Pyle pasture in the tall hills. Halfway up Clarot hill we came to where two canyons joined in the mountain. These canyons opened up onto a main canyon that ran down to the ranch.

The wolves had hidden in the draw where the two canyons ran into the large canyon. I looked in there and couldn't see anything. In our search we rode down right in the middle of the draw and then to the top of the canyon. Suddenly the white lobo got up within thirty feet of where we had passed by. We had passed close by and on three sides of the wolf without it being aware of us. To me, this indicated that it was both deaf and had no sense of smell or it would have scented us. It ran into the draw where there was a lot of brush. I only got a glimpse of it every once in a while. Even so, I took two shots at it and missed.

I told the doctor to stay on the top and I rode across the canyon which was about three quarter of a mile distance. When I got on the hill I saw it trotting along on a cow trail. I then got off my horse, took my gun and shot at her. She just stopped. I shot again and she fell over backward. The first shot killed her. The second one knocked her down. Both shots hit her in the heart just an inch away from each other. She was a fairly old female, all snow white, except a gray-tipped tail. Her tail was stiff as a board. She couldn't hear or smell, that's why I hadn't been able to catch her with scented and baited traps.

There was another smart lobo with which I had experience. A pack of lobos had just killed a calf. I immediately set and trapped one of the wolves that came back to eat from the carcass. The remainder of the pack I had to trail for three days. In that bunch was another wolf I tried to catch alive for T. M. Pyle and couldn't. I trailed it and finally found where it was laying up. When I got there the wolf left, but my little twenty-five- or thirty-pound fox terrier had a fresh trail to follow. The trail led to a canyon which was closed up with dead brush, so the wolf started up the hill. I saw it was a pretty smart animal as it went over the hill and under the first ledge which was about ten feet high. It came out and ran about two hundred yards when it ran by a prickly pear upon which the hook on the trap caught. The wolf then dragged the trap and chain back through so the hook came loose. It then made a dash through and got by and on out onto the top of the hill. By that time I was over there and I thought I would try to rope him. As my horse was afraid of it, I couldn't get close enough to rope him. Frustrated, I just got my gun, jumped off my horse and killed it. Upon examining this wolf, I found it didn't have any toes. Incidentally, I had caught him by the same foot from which a previous trap had gotten his toes. That was one reason he was smart. In addition, he had gotten to where he could get by with the trap and not get tangled up.

A big lobo on the Pyle Ranch was black on top and tan on its stomach. I happened onto it this way. A calf had been killed and I thought the black wolf did it. I set a trap at the kill and returned the next day with my fox terrier. The fox terrier discovered the wolf hung up by the trap and ran toward him. Before I could shoot the lobo it broke the hooks loose and was off. I followed. The fox terrier was much faster, caught up with him and jumped up and got his teeth right below the lobo's shoulder and hung on. The wolf was so pained and frightened that he ran for fifty yards and didn't even bite back at the terrier. I finally got on the other side of the wolf so I wouldn't shoot my dog and shot the wolf. The little terrier then ferociously jumped on the lobo's throat and thought he alone had killed the big animal.

After a lobo kills a calf, I can set my traps by the calf, because a wolf will come back to a kill. Lobos will eat meat that isn't fresh.

I set two traps by a calf that had been killed by a lobo and went back to the calf about daylight the next morning. My dog would run and scout around ahead of me. When my dog got to the calf he just sat down. I knew there was something wrong. He then got up and went about forty yards and stopped. I went over to him. There a coyote's head was sticking up out of the brush. A panther had killed it and after eating its hindquarters, had covered all of the coyote with grass and brush except its head. I went back to the calf and the panther had also covered its body with brush.

I got my dog on the panther's trail. It was a hot trail and the dog was in a hurry. The dog came to a high bluff. I had to help him up onto it. When on top, he saw the panther, ran after it and caught up with it and brought it to bay. In front of me was a large rock from which I expected the panther to jump off of and I would shoot him. Instead, he turned and went up the hill, making a fifteen-foot jump to the other ledge. I shot at him again and knocked one of his toes off. But when he got to the bottom of the hill he was dead. A panther will kill a coyote or a fox or anything like that. I don't think the panther ate any of the calf, having preferred the coyote.

A lobo would travel mostly at night, covering about twenty to twenty-five miles in twenty-four hours.

Lobos have a lonesome howl of a "yip-yap."

That concludes this particular narrative, but Wallace later related an interesting incident. One time he was three or four days late running his traps, and discovered one in which a lobo had been caught. The wolf had dragged the trap away. Upon following the trail of the lobo and trap, Montie found evidence that one or more lobos had brought meat for their trapped brother to eat. Not only do they engage in teamwork to catch prey, but use it to help preserve one another.

Around 1916, Walton Harral and his brothers of Fort Stockton caught two lobo pups from a wolf den, before their eyes were open. Like most baby animals, they were fed cow's milk and nursed on a bottle and nipple. The trappers, Doug Dean and one of the Hokit brothers, had dug deep into the soil around the den. They probably dug to a depth of ten or fifteen feet to catch those pups.

Though domesticated, the pups had to be tied up at the ripe old age of eight months. They were vicious to anyone except ranch personnel. Whenever they got loose they went on a killing rampage among the sheep and stock. Silver hairs scattered among their red coats gave them a grayish cast. Some wild animals, caught before their eyes are open and reared on a bottle, have some degree of tameness, but not those lobos.

Reportedly, lobos are now very scarce in this part of the Trans-Pecos country. Ted Gray of Alpine told me one lobo was killed northwest of Alpine last year. After discovering signs of its presence, the rancher drug a dead jackrabbit around, poisoned it and buried it in the vicinity. The next day, the dead lobo was found not far from the scene. Professional trappers would doubt the authenticity of that tale because of the wariness they attribute to lobos and the caution they insist must be taken to catch them.

Travis Roberts, of Brewster County, told me that in the Gage range of that county there is a new breed of the wolf, similar to the lobo in size but of a darker color. These wolves are depleting the deer and antelope on the Gage range, much as the lobo killed cattle in early days. As the game on the ranch furnishes part of the ranch income, the new wolves' ravages are a cost to the producing ability of that range, for the hunters pay for each deer they bag.

The Lynx and the Wildcat or Bobcat

The larger member of this variety of the cat family is the lynx, which generally weighs about fifty pounds. The wildcat/bobcat is about five or ten pounds lighter than the lynx.

The lynx, with longer legs and larger feet and claws, prefers a wooded region with trees to climb. The bobcat is usually found in areas with a lot of shrubbery, where it can more readily surprise rabbits, birds, rats, mice and other small game.

The bobcat (wildcat) is predominantly gray, with tawny

touches, and has more white under his belly. He is more spotted than the lynx. My friend, the true-life trapper, Charlie Stone, says the lynx is not only larger, but has longer tufts at the tips of its ears and longer whiskers.

Ranchers claim that the bobcat is more predominant in some areas, and the lynx is more predominant in other areas. Both cats have the characteristic habit of covering their excretion with sand. Trappers usually examine the sand and gravel deposits in arroyos when hunting for evidence of the cat's depredation. From this evidence, it can be determined just what the cat has been eating.

Like other felines, these two varieties want to stay close to water. The rancher's or farmer's poultry, small pigs, and other small or baby animals are favorite morsels for nearly all the cat family — sometimes even for the house cat.

In commenting about the lynx and the bobcat, the Judge included them as one and the same and wrote the following:

> It is a member of the cat family, which comprises all the carnivorous animals most formidable to man even now. They must have been still more dangerous to primitive man who was comparatively unarmed. As one evidence of the important position which felines held in the early history of man we may cite the permanence and widespread use of the name cat.
>
> The Greek name was "gata"; the Latin "catus"; the old French "cat"; the new French "chat"; the Danish "kat"; the Low German "katte"; the High German "katse"; the Irish "cat"; the Armenian "gitt". It is truly a name which has shown remarkable permanence of form and is evidenced by very widespread use.
>
> It is a notable example of a class of words from which an ingenious and entertaining theory sprung. This is the theory: All those nations using a term that is almost identical in form to designate the cat, are born from a common source and a common language — as distinct from nations which use a radically different term to designate the animal. Hence, nations

which use identical terms are called "Aryan" nations. It has been argued, from a variety of peculiar facts and inferences that the original home of the ancestral nation was in far off Persia, in a province called Arya. The site of this ancestral home of the so-called "Aryan" language has been much disputed. Various authors placed it in different locales. There is general agreement that all nations which exhibit a great number of words of essentially similar structure in their languages are descended from a people who used a common language — and that these ancestors must have lived in Western Asia or Central Europe.

The Mexican name, "gato de montes," includes two words, one of which illustrates the susceptibility of words to change meaning during the course of centuries of use. "Gato" has suffered little change of form and none of meaning for thousands of years. The Spaniards derived "montes" from the Latin language, in its original form. Among the Romans, it meant "mountains" — an English word derived from it which shows greater variation in spelling from the original than the Spanish term. In the Roman countries, mountains were almost always wooded, and when the word passed to the Spanish, it had a secondary meaning. A "gato de montes" would mean a "cat of the forest." With this meaning attached, the word was brought to Spanish America. But in America — particularly where the Spanish landed in Mexico — mountains were more often bare. The word now has a tertiary meaning — that of a bare and wild district. It carries that meaning today, and when the Mexicans call our lynx a "gato de montes," the phrase signifies much the same as our wildcat.

Now we take our word lynx and find it to be a Greek word, almost as old as the hills. It was also used in early Greek days as a man's name, just as bear and wolf were used among the Anglo Saxons. Thus, among the Argonauts who sailed under Jason to get the Golden Fleece, there was a warrior named Lynx, who was distinguished for his remarkable eyesight. From him comes the phrase "lynx-eyed" and not from any extraordinary power of vision in our animal. So far as I can ascertain the lynx has no better or keener power of sight than the coyote or other wild animals, and is inferior to the hawk or turkey buzzard in that respect. However, the notion prevails that it has extraordinary eyesight. I think this opinion is wholly due to the phrase "lynx-eyed," and the common impression that the figure of speech refers to the animal. If so it is a very apt example of the "propter hoc" argument based on a "post hoc" fact.

I find the name of Lucifer Cats frequently applied to these animals in the Canadas and British North America. I am at a loss to understand the appropriateness of this name. Lucifer means "light-bearing" and is properly used in the term Lucifer matches. The Romans used this word to denote the morning star. I do not understand how this cat can be "light-bearing," unless it refers to the brilliancy of its eyes and its habit of prowling in the dark.

Isaiah refers to "Lucifer, son of the morning" in such a way that the name has been generally accepted as equivalent to that of Satan, chief of fallen angels, and great enemy of man. Here again, I can find nothing symbolical of the character of the archenemy in the lynx. Certainly the cat could not be compared to a fallen angel, and it is not as destructive and dangerous an enemy to man as many other wild beasts. And Satan is never featured as being bob-tailed!

Of all the species of the cat family, this is the only one of recognized standing that rejoices in an abbreviated tail. To be sure there is the Manx variety of our domestic cat, but that discredited and bastard member of the tribe of house-cats is apparently a cross from the lynx. All the other branches of the family are possessed of long and very flexible tails, but the lynx is the aristocratic and exclusive possessor of a very short, rigid and stubby final ending. Nature economized for some good reason, for the tail seems to be of little use to the cat family.

The lynx has not cut an outstanding figure among animal life in Pecos County. Twenty-five years ago it was probably more numerous than it is today, but it represents no danger to the cattle industry, and does little damage to sheep as long as they are herded. Consequently it has received none of those flattering but dangerous considerations from men which have distinguished the career of the lobo and puma. It is occasionally hunted with hounds, for the pleasure of the chase, and to train the dogs to chase pumas. I recall no successful attempts to poison it. Ranchmen consider it with good natured contempt, too unimportant to justify much trouble or effort to exterminate it.

I must digress from the Judge's narrative to further explain his statement that the lynx or wildcat "does little damage to sheep as long as they are herded. . . ." Occasionally a sheep or lamb wandered some distance from the flock, the herder and the dog. Under these circumstances, a cat could and would kill it. In addition, herders built a brush corral in which the sheep were placed at night. This provided some protection against predators, especially when lanterns were placed around it and baited traps were set nearby. Otherwise, the cats were a problem at night even if the herder had a dog. Judge Williams continues:

> It sometimes arouses the ire of the good housewife, for it is a dangerous enemy of poultry and small barnyard animals, all of which lie within the housewife's sphere of industry. In the wild, its chief prey is birds, rabbits, prairie dogs and small game. It takes very quickly to catching small domestic animals, and once it gets in that habit it must be hunted down, for it will not return to its former habit of hunting wild prey.
>
> For many years it was almost impossible to successfully raise poultry on the Rooney and 7D ranches near Fort Stockton due to the ravages of the lynx. At one time, the Rooney ranch had a large adobe corral, seven feet high, around the headquarters, yet a cat has been known to jump over this wall in daylight, and seize a large turkey by the neck, jump back over the wall, and escape to its lair with its prey. I have often thought

that it was the old animals which do the most damage to domestic farm animals, because they're grown too feeble to catch wild prey. This cat which leaped a seven foot wall and back again with its prey in its mouth was no feeble old animal. It was probably a young animal in its prime.

Like all of the cat tribe, it is unable to live far from water. Its favorite haunts in this area have been along the banks of the Pecos River and up and down small creeks. It was the man-made canals running through the Rooney and 7D ranches which opened up new territory to the animal. These canals enabled it to live near the ranches and become so destructive to the ranchers. Marshes and tules make good hiding for it and it frequently hides in cultivated crops. When Mr. T. J. Ray established his irrigated farm in this county in 1891, at Santa Rosa, he cultivated sorghum, sowed broadcast, for several years. After the plant had grown up high enough to shelter them, these patches of sorghum became the home of the big cats. At almost any hour of the day or night a trip to the sorghum patch would rouse one or more of them. They foraged on Mr. Ray's domestic animals from this shelter until he found it necessary to cease raising sorghum.

It has five or six cubs per litter, and in actions, voice and appearance, the young remind one very much of domestic kittens. They are quite light colored — even yellow — when small, but grow darker as they get older. They have often been caught when small and raised as pets and proved to be very gentle and playful nearly up to maturity. But on attaining full growth, the wild instincts and habits surface, and it becomes a very dangerous neighbor to poultry and small domestic animals.

Many years ago a small lynx was raised in the town of Fort Stockton. It belonged to Mr. John Lemons. [At that time the John Lemons family lived in the building which later housed the Gray Mule Saloon.] The lynx was a female, was very playful, and seemed to know everybody in town. It had a habit of hiding behind the door and then appearing suddenly, which always frightened small boys and seemed to greatly amuse the animal. It became the property of Mr. George Hawthorne when it was nearly grown and was removed to Sanderson, in Terrell County, where Mr. Hawthorne was then residing. Its new owner was very fond of a good joke, and derived much amusement in various ways.

A well-known Chinaman named Sam Sing had a restaurant near the spot where the lynx was kept fastened at the end of a long chain. Sam's business required a great many chickens and turkeys and he kept a number of them in a large hen house. Occasionally, they were allowed to roam around and pick up a living on the outside, and were thereby brought within reach of our cat. When Mr. Hawthorne saw some of the fowls approaching, he would call his friends to watch the fun. He would sprinkle some corn on the ground around the cat and stand aside to await the rush of the fowls. The cat gauged the length of her chain very accurately. She never made a rush when the fowl was beyond her reach.

She would lie still, head resting on forepaws, her eyes closed — feigning a good nap. But as soon as an unfortunate fowl was safely within the length of her chain, she pounced. She would trot serenely back to her box with her prey, and proceed to dine royally. It was all done so demurely and yet so certainly, that it became regular sport for its owner and his friends. The sport came to an untimely end when Sam Sing gravely presented a bill for 27 chickens, sundry turkeys and other fowl, to Mr. Hawthorne. Thereafter our cat did not dine so luxuriously.

Due to the ease with which a young lynx may be brought up tame, it is probable that it would long ago have been domesticated, but for the difficulty of getting it to serve any useful purpose. Possibly, it was more difficult to domesticate our common cat than the lynx. But the tame cat has learned to preserve a fairly reverent aspect towards its ability and disposition to catch and destroy rats, mice, snakes and other animals noxious to man. It has proven valuable, so that the time and patience necessarily employed in rooting out its habits of catching poultry have been persistently followed by man. And as this time and patience has been employed to protect the larger fowls, the instinct of the animal to catch birds and very small fowl remains very much in evidence to this day.

I must disagree with the Judge this time regarding the ease with which a young lynx may be tamed. To my knowledge, he apparently never had that experience.

Our neighbors, the late Hood Mendels, had a tame lynx. The Mendels told me it wouldn't bite, but when I visited them, it made me very nervous. The lynx hungrily ran its teeth over my arm. Later, I heard that Mr. Mendel was rudely awakened from his noonday nap by the lynx which was chewing on his ear — in spite of assurances that it wouldn't bite. That was the end of that easily tamed pet. The Judge continues:

> Due to its large size, the lynx would not be very successful in catching small vermin. Apparently, it is not very useful to man, and that is probably why no effort was made to domesticate it. Every domestic animal brought under man's dominion has cost some primitive tribe a high price in patience and trouble. Such labor will not be employed without a useful end in view. Perhaps some of those animals which perished from the earth might have proven more valuable than anything we have. We will never know about this, but we may be sure that animals were domesticated with a serviceable end in mind. Since the lynx does not seem to present any hope of useful service, it may eventually perish as a breed.
>
> The process of weeding out useless animals continues with the centuries. As there are no human means available to create new species of animals, the world consequently grows poorer in varieties of animal life. This is inevitable. The only compensation we find is that the animals which we choose to remain

with us are bred into widely divergent breeds, possessing beauty and usefulness which were undreamed of by those savages who had the foresight to commence the process of domesticating them.

In the process of evolution it may be that our race will even begin to cull out domesticated animals, and will allow some of them to perish. It is not difficult to imagine that the time may yet come when there are no domestic animals, and man will live, act, and almost think, purely by mechanical devices. Where will our nature lover be then?

My friend, the lifelong trapper Charlie Stone, made the following comments about bobcats:

> Bobcats are usually easy to catch. You just have to find out what run he makes. A bobcat has a run it will follow for a week or two weeks or a month. If you find out his run you'll catch him eventually. A bobcat usually runs in a draw or canyons or the rimrock.
> When a bobcat kills a sheep, it grabs the sheep by the neck and cuts its throat. A coyote usually kills a sheep by the throat, but sometimes when it's running it will catch a sheep by the backend.
> You can catch a bobcat by putting a roadrunner by the trap, or a rabbit tail hanging from the bush by a string. A red bird is good bait. Anything that will attract them. I've pulled some tricks on bobcats. I used to catch a lot of big ole wildcats.
> Once I was in the Davis Mountains and I caught a big old wildcat. I thought I'd have some fun. So I got some bailing wire and wrapped it around the wildcat's neck real fast and stretched him out real tight and put my foot on his neck and [one by one] wired up his paws.
> I asked my wife to come help me tie down the wildcat and she came over and when she got there, I let the wildcat go and scared my wife to death. She ran off down the hill. When it was over, boy, she was real mad! She didn't know it couldn't hurt her because it was completely wired up.

I've had dogs chase a cat up a tree and I'd try and punch it out with a stick. Sometimes they give pretty good battles and other times pretty good horse chases.

One time Mr. J. E. Hill and I went cat hunting on the Cunningham ranch [twelve miles east of Fort Stockton]. Hill had three Walker hounds, one of which always wandered off. Soon this hound jumped a cat and run the dickens out of him. Mr. Hill was farther away and went over to where he heard the hounds.

Because it was pretty cold I went under the cover of an overhanging ledge. There I found a couple of bobcat kittens. I got up pretty close to them and was bending over to see them better when the hound chased that cat down over the ledge. The cat didn't know I was in there. As the cat didn't have time to look, it jumped off of that ledge or boulder onto my back. I got out of there fast — nearly tore that mountain down! That cat also took out of there. It ran about a mile and went into some caves. We never did catch him.

The wildcat will stay with its kittens till they're old enough to catch rats and rabbits. Wildcats usually have their dens in the cliffs or caves. Sometimes, when a river washes up enough dead brush they might have their kittens in there. Or sometime, an old tree might fall down and they would live in the brush around it.

I know of a wildcat now that's sixteen years old. It was caught as a kitten sixteen years ago and it's still alive.

Sometimes I catch a bobcat and stretch him out and tie all his feet and take him home for the pups to chase. That's a good way to teach pups to hunt. We let the older hounds go with the little ones so the pups know what all the barking is about. Once I had a bobcat jump on the back of my dog and ride him like a horse for about thirty feet and then he fell off. You train a dog not to chase any animal except the animal you're hunting. If you're hunting cat and the dog chases coyote you've got to whup it out of him. The dogs are trained to chase one animal. Sometimes it takes a good doubled-up rope to train one and if he won't learn you've got to kill him. But you can train one if you've got patience and a good dog to go with him. When you hunt bear or panther you use bloodhounds because they can pick up an older trail. That's called a cold nose dog because he can pick up a colder trail.

My own experience with the lynx and the wildcat is limited to the knowledge of the stock loss they inflicted on me. I managed to get someone else to trap predators, and cats were among that class, especially on my Angora goats.

In a pasture four miles west of Fort Stockton, I stocked nanny goats to eat out the "yellow weed." While doing this, I wanted them to pay their way partially by producing offspring and mohair. I always noticed one old nanny grazing at the same spot, near a grove of hackberry trees. One day she was missing.

A search in the nearby brush revealed the carcass of my nanny goat. The meat was eaten from around her neck and flank. The tracks around the carcass were those of a lynx and its little ones. My foreman, the late Frank Edwards, set a trap. The next morning I found the cat about one hundred yards away, where it had dragged the trap after being caught. We poisoned the goat's carcass in hopes of catching the little lynxes.

The late J. E. Hill, frequently referred to by Charlie Stone, trapped for me during the latter years of his life. Both cats and coyotes did extensive damage to our two thousand head of sheep. Mr. Hill was setting traps on the west line of my range in the brush of Acibuche Draw.

This typical frontiersman, a product of the plains area, was six feet, five inches tall, dark and handsome. He had spent his life trapping, and for many years he was head of the predator trappers of Pecos County. At the time he trapped for me he had had several severe heart attacks and was bothered by chronic heart trouble. His doctor advised that his wife be with him when he made his rounds to investigate his traps. She was assigned the lifting or any heavy work. Mrs. Hill was her husband's opposite — short, chunky, and somewhat talkative.

One day, after they had returned from our ranch, Mr. Hill was lying in bed when I stopped by to get his report. With a twinkle in his eye, he told me this story:

"When we got to the location of the trap in the brushy part of Acibuche Draw, it was gone. So the wife took the .22 rifle and led the way following the prints on the weed and brush of the dragged trap. All of a sudden the trapped cat jumped out at her and she dropped that gun and nearly tore all of her clothes off of her as she ran through the catclaw and brush."

Mrs. Hill, standing nearby, was not amused by her husband's tale, and loudly proclaimed, "That's a damn lie!"

And maybe it was! Regardless, Mr. Hill enjoyed telling the story, and embellishing the details of his wife's reaction to a sudden face-to-face confrontation with a lynx.

I quote my old friend, Tom Moore, who was quite a hunter and lover of hound dogs:

> In a way a coon is smarter than a coyote or a wildcat. But in another way I think a bobcat is the smartest. I've run a bobcat for an hour watching him on the ledges, seeing how he moves. He'll be up on the bluffs with about four different levels. The bobcat will be on one level, and the dogs on one below. When the dogs get on a level where they can get him, he jumps down to a lower level.
>
> My wife, Myrtle, and I ran [one] for three hours one time, [just] watching him. We never did shoot him. The dogs wore him out. We had some good dogs. Wildcats are hard to catch, for the most part. Old cats get pretty smart.
>
> On Jim Deacon's ranch, near Pecos, I remember we would go out there every week to catch it [a certain wildcat]. One night we had chased it for an hour when the dogs bayed and they had "treed it"

on a hackberry tree about seven feet tall. The cat [on a limb] was low enough that we could catch him. We had chased him so many times I wanted to kill him.

But Ernest [Riggs] said, "Doggone! Don't kill him. Let's knock him out and let the dogs kill him [while we watch the fight]." So he pulled out a wrench from his [automobile] pocket, reached up there and hit him. When he did, the cat jumped as far as he could right through those dogs and ran a ways and then hid behind a bush.

The dogs were going so fast, following the leader, they ran right past that bobcat and went on a ways. The cat backtracked off somewhere else. Then we chased [around for] him for about two hours, but never got the trail again.

Tom's cat was one of those old smart, experienced cats! Ernest Riggs of Fort Stockton enjoyed telling a story about one of his hunts. One of the members of this party was my old friend, the late Dan Patterson. Patterson had been a blacksmith in his youth and was known to be strong and handy with his fists. It was said that he was a man who could "whip his weight in wildcats."

Reportedly, he was the only man in Pecos County who ever challenged the tough, dangerous, Sheriff "Dud" Barker. Although Barker was a good law enforcement officer, he had quite a temper and had engaged in the killing of a number of men — supposedly twenty-two. Nevertheless, Patterson told Barker that if Barker would drop his gun, he (Patterson) would whip hell out of him. This challenge to a formidable law officer from a one-eyed man (Patterson had one glass eye) had earned Dan Patterson quite a reputation. The following story told by Ernest Riggs enhanced it considerably.

Ernest said the dogs had treed a wildcat or lynx in an old cottonwood tree on the 7D farms about three miles east of Fort Stockton. When the hounds bayed, all of the hunters started converging at that sound. Ernest and Dan were together, struggling through the brush at night. That was difficult enough for Ernest, but it was more so for Dan with only one good eye.

When they reached the scene where the hounds had the cat treed, Dan's clothes were badly torn, and he was covered with blood from various cuts and scratches. The other members of the hunt did not arrive for some time. Dan climbed the tree, went out on the limb where the cat was sitting — and the cat jumped. Dan descended safely to the ground. The dogs ripped into the cat furiously, as the other hunters began to arrive.

There stood Dan, who had taken his glass eye out and was calmly cleaning it with a bloody handkerchief. Dan was never modest about that eye. His clothes were in tatters; his face and hands, and his one good eye were covered with blood. The other wide-eyed members of the hunt asked Ernest, "What happened?"

Ernest replied, "Well, old Dan just went up that tree like a monkey, caught that cat by the neck, and brought it down and handed it to the dogs."

Because of Dan's reputation, and his appearance, the other hunters believed what Ernest told them. That just shows you what the right kind of reputation can do for you.

Dan's reputation was well earned and his courage unquestionable. After this incident he became legendary. A good or a bad reputation generally grows to astonishing lengths. In the imagination of the people of Pecos County, Dan's courage grew by leaps and bounds. It far exceeded that of the East Texas man who climbed a tree expecting to push a possum off a limb. Instead of a possum, so the story goes, he met a wildcat face to face; and when the cat started clawing up and down the man's front side, he shouted down to his friends: "Just shoot up amongst us. It don't make any difference which one of us is hit!"

The Ring-Tailed Cat and the Raccoon
(Bassariscus and Procyon lotor)

The Genus Bassariscus, or the ring-tailed cat, ranges from Oregon, Colorado and Texas to southern Mexico. They are not as common along the southern area of the Pecos River as the Procyon lotor, a species which exists in most areas of the United States, and from Canada to Central America.

But the ring-tailed raccoon prefers rocky, rough places, near water. His ringed tail is about seventeen and a half inches long (much longer than our regular raccoon), and it is banded with black and white rings. This type makes his den up in the rock crevices, hollow trees, and similar places. From May to June, they have one to five cubs. For the first three weeks of the cubs' life only the mother cares for them. Thereafter, both parents provide food for the little ones. At four months the cubs are weaned, and they are about adult size when they reach four and one-half months. I am told that these ring-tailed cats have a piercing bark and will let forth a scream. As far as I know, I've never heard one.

The color of the Procyon lotor ranges from gray to almost black. They have from five to ten rings on their furry black tails. They also have black streaks across their broad heads and have sharp pointed muzzles. The head of this species appears somewhat "foxy." They have long toes on their front feet which can be spread apart and used like fingers. The two classes of raccoons are both nocturnal, are similar in size, and have much the same habits.

Both types of animals will raid the rancher's and farmer's chicken pens. They also eat plants, small mammals, insects, and birds. They are particularly fond of catching minnows and small fish. Charlie Stone said: "Some people catch coons by setting a trap in the water with foil or something shiny on the pedal and the raccoon goes to see what it is and gets caught."

Judge Williams wrote:

> When I was a boy, growing up in the Mississippi Valley, I had some limited experience in chasing coons. However, small boys rarely consider their experiences to be limited. I had the advantage of being acquainted with many schoolboy "chums" who were full of lore on "coon" hunts. They were also eager to impart such information to their credulous companions. In due time, I began to regard myself as an expert on the customs of the raccoon. Perhaps unconsciously I mentally assembled the following cir-

cumstances as necessary concomitants for the presence of the raccoon in a given geographical area.

The first requirement is permanent water in the immediate neighborhood of its domicile. Second, there must be a wooded area along the banks of the water. This must consist of relatively large trees of the size, age and kind to furnish hollow logs or stumps in which the animal can make its den; or with roots under which the raccoon can burrow out a lair. Fourth, in the event of an emergency, no well-mannered coon with any prestige among his peers would take up residence in any locale where he could not take his last stand among the high branches of some lofty tree, or in the middle of a deep pool or small lake. For me, the words of the old Negro song, "Cooney up a gum-stump, possum in de holler," localized the coon as appropriately as a polar bear is depicted on an iceberg.

In time, [1884] I came to Pecos County. Here was a vast arid country with great stretches of territory that were barren of surface water. If I may be permitted a slight hyperbole, a thin thread of water known as the Pecos River flowed along the north and east sides of the county. For 300 miles, not a tree stood along the banks of this river. The area was happily distinguished by three small oases. A small spring gushed from under a ledge of limestone rock and ran for about three miles at the Tunas headland. At Leon Springs a vast well rose up in the marshes and tules and sent its surplus waters bubbling down a small channel for four or five miles through the open plain. Magnificent Comanche Creek marked the site of the third oasis. Crystal clear water came up in the hollow of a wide, treeless plain and flowed away from the flag at the old fort for some 10 or 12 miles, to be dissipated in the earth and air. For approximately 8,000 square miles around the waters, and the vast plains that lay between, nothing grew that could be dignified by the name, tree — save a few cottonwoods recently transplanted by man within the irrigated areas of Leon and Comanche Creeks. In some spots, a low, sparse scattered growth of insignificant shrubs pretended to hide the bosom of the earth from the glare of the sun, but over the majority of the land, even this thin veil was lacking, and the earth lay bare under the scalding heat of the desert sun.

At first sight, these surface conditions were so far removed from those ideal concomitants that I mentally associated with the raccoon, that I did not even so much as think of coons. My surprise was great when I learned that the "Little Brother to the Bear," as the Algonquins call him, was an inhabitant of Pecos County. True, the animal was confined to narrow, well defined areas, but it was found in comparative abundance within those areas. Within a mile's distance of the water, considerable numbers of raccoons were found along the Pecos River, and along Leon and Comanche Creeks. It was rarely, if ever, found out of that limited belt of country. The earliest white visitor had found it in the same numbers.

I had to amend my previous expert opinions as to the habitat of the coon. Evidently it could dispense with the woods and trees to use as a hiding place and home. It still must stay near water, which seems indispensable to it. It must have water to drink, and unique to most animals, the coon has a curious habit of washing all of its food before eating it. In this country, the animal depends upon water to furnish almost its entire diet. It catches the fish, frogs, snakes, snails, and various insects and small animals, which in turn, depend upon the water for their existence.

For its lair, it can and does follow the example of the coyote and the badger and digs a hole in the ground. This den is a nest for its young, and a city of refuge when the animal is pursued. We have cracks in the earth, like the cracks in the famous "black waxy" prairies of old time Texas. These breaks are found in the borders of the marshes and along the margins of the creeks and river. They are quite deep and ragged in places and have probably been caused by the land drying out after high water and overflow. Such spots are favorite haunts of the coon in the daytime, and he often hollows them out and shapes them into a home.

Comanche and Leon Creeks are not far apart and run parallel to one another. The coon can now pass from one valley to the other by following irrigation ditches. Before the existence of these ditches, passage from the water in one valley, to the water in the other one was considerably more difficult for the animal. However, if he could get to one valley, we can easily understand how he could get to the other. What is difficult for me to understand is how the animal could have gotten to this area to begin with, from a place where it could have lived and thrived. When we find an animal abundant in a place that is apparently isolated and unapproachable by its kin, we naturally speculate upon its origin in that area. It is apparent there must have been some cause for the coon's existence in this area which is not covered by the ordinary course of events.

We may designate Leon and Comanche Creeks as the Fort Stockton District. This district is very much isolated from any other surface water. It is more than 40 miles from water to water on the west and south. As mentioned before, Tunas Spring lies 19 miles to the east. It is the nearest permanent water to the Stockton District water, but it is yet 20 miles from the Pecos River. On the north, the two creeks, Leon and Comanche, lose themselves in wide flats 10 or 15 miles from Fort Stockton, where they appear for the last time. From these last evidences of water it is yet some 25 miles to the next water, which is the Pecos River. The animal is found up and down this river and may have been found there as long as the river has flowed. The coon most probably came to the Fort Stockton District from the river if we are to judge the probabilities from present conditions.

But how did it cross the intermediate country? This area is a flat plain, destitute of water. Even now it has little brush to form covert, and it was much more barren 50 years ago, if we may judge from the reports of travelers. It has nothing in the way of food to entice the animal from its haunts on the river. This would appear a totally effective barrier to an animal of the coon's habits. Fish, frogs and water snails also exist in these isolated creeks, but there is an adequate explanation for their transport to these waters. It is a well known and well authenticated fact that water birds carry the eggs and spawn of these creatures in their feathers and in the mud on their feet from one water to another, thus aiding in the spread of these species to previously unoccupied localities. No such explanation can be given for the spread of a mammal.

I have heard three theories advanced to account for the presence of the animal in such an isolated place as the Fort Stockton District, where it apparently could not have arrived without the aid of some other power as the country now stands. One of these is a very speculative one, leading back into a remote past. At best, it is simply a suggestion of a possibility, but as each theory either takes into consideration the physical formation of this section, or derives its probability from circumstances in the early history of the country, it may prove of some interest to recite them. Such speculations often give one a better and more vivid idea of a country and its history, than could be impressed by a careful and detailed, but prosaic statement of facts.

The first theory assumes that the animal was brought here by the white man. Over a period of about 400 years, both Spaniard and American visited Comanche Creek many times before its final settlement by the Americans. Cabeza de Vaca and three comrades passed through this area in 1536. We know that in 1584, Espejo traveled down the Pecos River and crossed to Presidio del Norte with his Spanish soldiers. Later some priests went from Presidio to the Indians dwelling near the present site of San Angelo. Each of these parties probably passed through the Fort Stockton District, judging the probabilities by the topography and accessibility to water in this area. In 1839, an American merchant of Chihuahua, named Connelly, took a large freight train from Chihuahua to the United States. He made the return trip in 1841, and used Comanche Creek as a station on both the outward and the return journey. In 1849, soldiers began passing through on their way to guard the frontier, and emigrants headed for the gold fields of California. This migration continued until a permanent military post was established at Fort Stockton in about 1854 [1859].

There was ample opportunity for the white man to introduce the coon into the fauna of the Fort Stockton District, but there is absolutely no evidence indicating that this was what happened. Actually there are several facts weighing against the probability.

First, the coon was as numerous in the district in 1855 as it is now. Soldiers, stage drivers and others who were here in those days confirm this fact. An old traveler's account, written during that period of time, also mentions the coon. Consequently, it was introduced prior to 1850, and prior to that time white men were not often in this district. With the exception of Connelly's train, it is unlikely that those who did pass through here would encumber themselves with a pair of coons. They certainly would not have brought them for the express purpose of stocking the country. To me, this theory seems very improbable.

Another theory gives the Indian credit for introducing the coon. This is a much more credible theory. In pre-settler days, Apaches occupied the Fort Stockton District. There is much evidence to verify this. Their peculiar graves are found up and down Comanche and Leon Creeks, and there are many deeply bored "metate" holes formed in rock at various points along Comanche Creek. I have seen some of these holes which were so large and so deeply bored into the rock that I think it must have required 50 years' use to wear one to its present dimensions. The burned remains of their rock stoves and cooking places are frequently found. All of this shows an occupation which was perhaps desultory and broken, but nevertheless extended over a long series of years.

Like all primitive tribes, the Indians were very fond of having animal pets. The coon was a favorite, and common in the households of the Southern Indians. In his Neufragios, in 1535, Cabeza de Vaca mentions that the Indians near the Gulf of Mexico had many voiceless dogs. There is a general belief that this description represented tamed coons. If the animal did not arrive in this area by its own unaided efforts, then it is quite possible that it did come as an escaped pet of the Apaches.

The last theory gives the coon credit for finding its way into our country without having to pass the barren and waterless wasteland which now stands in its way. However — it throws the time of the animal's coming so far back in the past that an entirely different environment existed in what is now Pecos County. In fact, we must roll time back to a period when the high level of the old cretaceous formation still stood over most of this country — when that high level remained still curving in a high front of semi-circular form, running from the 7D Mountain to the south first and then to the west, ending in what is now the high rampart of the Twelve Mile Mountain, while on a lower level, but much higher than they now stand, the Comanche Springs broke out in the center of that primeval amphitheatre.

It is said that in those faraway days, the Pecos River had not yet cut its deep serpentine course through the cretaceous hills lying between Sheffield and the Rio Grande River, but was dammed back while its waters formed a long lake running back a great distance and covered much of the country between Fort Stockton and the Pecos River now lying in the Gibson and Baldridge Ranch. The water of Comanche Creek poured directly into this lake. Under these circumstances the coon had no difficulty in establishing residence on the Creek.

In the course of time, the river eroded a deeper and deeper channel in the rocks about Sheffield, and the lake grew ever smaller. Finally, there was nothing left but the river cutting its path through the floor of the old lake bed. In the meantime, the rainfall decreased and the country grew more and more arid —

until finally the barren, waterless wasteland between the Pecos River and the lower springs of Comanche Creek grew to be 25 miles wide. During this period coons on Comanche Creek were cut off from communication with their brethren on the Pecos River. Becoming a law unto themselves, they ceased to follow some of the customs, habits and manners of ancestors in "the good old days." Now they are characterized by some aspects that are quite different from the parent race.

It is said that these Comanche Creek animals are colored and marked differently from the standard coon of the United States. I understand that they also fail to follow the time-honored practice of paying special attention to hen roosts — and it is even claimed that they have no particular fondness for roasting ears. I cannot vouch for the assertion about color and marking, nor about their lack of taste for good chickens, but I have raised corn in the midst of numerous coons, and have yet to observe any signs of their raiding in the field. I am inclined to think that the isolation of the animal over a period of years has educated it to use a fish and frog diet more exclusively than its brethren in more favored localities. This hermit community is tied to the margin of two small creeks and for untold eons, the coon found its sole livelihood from the natural products of those small streams. In the course of passing centuries it lost the instincts and inherited knowledge which led it to seek other food. It is no more a pest to the farmers who have moved in on its ancient domain than it is to the farmers 1,000 miles away from its little fringe of land and water.

A very successful farmer, McAteer, lived on the Acibuche Draw. He reported that he allowed a Mexican laborer on his place to plant a few acres in a truck garden for home consumption. The laborer first attempted to grow a garden along a country highway. This site was robbed of its ripe melons by some two-legged night prowlers. The location of the garden was changed from the road to a place near the draw.

Again night prowlers robbed him of his ripe melons and corn. It was discovered that these prowlers were raccoons. Despite the fact that the melons were covered over with heavy brush, the raccoons pulled aside the limbs of the brush, dug a hole into the melon and took what they wanted of the melon meat. They never punctured a melon that was not ripe.

One summer when I operated our farm and ranch properties, we had harvested and shocked a large supply of hegari to use for winter stock feed. Hegari stalks are bound in bundles and tied with wire or stout twine. These bundles are stacked in the form of a cone which is called a feed shock. It resembles a small teepee. When men with trucks were sent to load the bundles and haul the feed away, they found that many raccoons had made their homes inside these shocks of feed where they had both food and shelter. In addition to feasting on the grain, the coons could catch the different birds and animals which came to feed upon the hegari, such as field mice.

When I was but a lad, I sometimes followed hunting dogs down Comanche Creek. One day I heard some dogs which sounded as though they were in abject misery down toward the old dam. When I arrived at the scene, an outnumbered raccoon was giving three or four dogs an exceedingly bad time. While Mr. Coon swam merrily around in the middle of the creek, the dogs would attempt to bite him. When an unfortunate dog got close enough, the coon would push the canine's head under the water, proceed to climb on top of the dog's head and leap from that vantage point to the top of another dog's head. He was about to succeed in drowning all of the dogs before they gave up the chase.

Apparently my boyhood experience was not a once-in-a-lifetime coon event. Charlie Stone experienced a similar happening. Charlie told me that he, Tom Moore and a few other men followed their dogs on foot as the dogs trailed a raccoon for three or four miles. Either the dogs had closed in on the raccoon, or it had waited for them at a deep stock tank located about four or five miles northwest of Fort Stockton, a few miles west of the Paul Crone place. Evidently the coon had swum out into the middle of the pool as soon as the dogs closed in on it. It was exerting great effort to drown all the dogs. That raccoon was leaping agilely from the head of one dog to the head of another. When it would land on one dog's head, the coon would hold him under until the dog was gasping and nearly done for — then he would jump to the head of the canine coming to the rescue of his compatriot.

At this point, the men arrived on the scene. Tom Moore shucked his clothing and waded out to rescue the floundering dogs. He swung his fist against that coon a couple of times, grabbed it by the tail and swung it in circles above his head until he reached the shore and then threw it out on the land where the dogs finished it off.

Tom Moore elaborated on this dog-drowning phenomenon. He told me the following:

> I've had to jump in the water several times to get my dogs away from the coons. Riggs and I did that at a big water tank at his place while the late Dr. Sibley, Sr. owned it. We had a big coon out in the middle of a deep tank. We had four or five dogs that night and that coon was about to drown them dogs. He'd get on top of their heads and on their backs and the dogs would go under. We had to jump in there and save those dogs.
>
> I've trapped lots of coons. Ordinarily I used a Newhouse No. 4 trap — the same as I'd used for coyote. But when I trap especially for coons, I use a No. 3. When you catch a coon in the big traps if it doesn't have an offset jaw, it [the coon] will chew its foot off and get away. Coons sometimes stray a long ways from water. When the mesquite beans are

green and ripe, you can find one [a raccoon] ten miles from water.

Relative to the sport of hunting raccoons, Tom said:

> I've had several good coon dogs. The best story I've heard, wasn't [on] me, it was on Pockets [a younger brother, John], and John Dees. Pockets was a lad and wanted to go with John Dees, who had some black and tan coon dogs and went down to the creek every weekend and hunted coons. Pockets' job was to carry a stick and when the dogs ran a coon up a tree he'd [climb up and] knock it out and the dogs would get it.
>
> [One time at night] they saw a couple of dogs baying at something but weren't catching it even though it was on the ground. Pockets decided he'd go knock that coon on the head. When he got there it was a skunk. Thereafter for some time, young Pockets and his striped coon both reeked of the same perfume.

I have seen only a few pet raccoons. Reportedly, when they get old they become irritable and difficult to handle. On one occasion a friend and I were returning from a convention. The friend had a hangover from consuming too much alcohol. He managed to find a shack with a bed in it in which to recuperate before arriving home. He hit the bed immediately and fell fast asleep while I sat in a rocking chair and read a periodical.

A bold raccoon, which apparently was or had been somebody's pet, entered the room through a broken window, spotted the languid body of my inebriated friend, and made himself at home. The animal searched through the pockets of the man's pants, and then stood on my friend's chest, surveying the situation. Uncertain just what to do, the coon stuffed a front foot in each of my friend's ears. That awoke the gentleman — who had fully expected to see pink elephants or snakes at any time. When he discovered the

"Little Brother to the Bear" staring him right in the face, it was too much. Both animal and human took off. The startled raccoon sped out the window from whence it came, and my frightened friend nearly tore down the door.

The Fox
(Vulpes macrotis)

Scientists tell us there are seven species of red foxes (genus Vulpes) in North America north of Mexico, Europe, most of Africa and most of Asia. The American red fox, Vulpes vulpas fulva, is said to be a subspecies. The Vulpes velox and Vulpes macrotis inhabit the western half of the Great Plains from southwestern Canada into Texas and northern Mexico.

The animal is the size of a small dog and has a pointed nose and ears. Its round bushy tail is as long as the head and body combined. Like the skunk and badger, most foxes have glands under their tails that secrete a repulsive odor.

Foxes are not particular about their diet. They eat most anything, including rats, mice, fruits, berries, insects, lizards and snails. They even dig out the tuna and pitahaya fruit with their fingerlike front claws.

Like wolves, foxes are believed to mate for life. Late winter or early spring is their mating time, after which the female either digs her own den or takes over an abandoned hole. The den has several entrances.

While looking for the bones of kid goats and sheep, C. R. McKenzie dug out a fox hole. He found a large den about five feet underground with three separate holes leading to it. Possibly three differently located holes indicate that the fox had a planned escape route. C. R. found no evidence of goat or sheep bones, but he did find plenty of signs of snakes, rats, birds, rabbits, lizards and mice. Once you have tampered with a den, the foxes will leave and not return to it.

Inside the den there is an additional chamber to store food, which also serves as a nursery for the cubs. The litter generally includes five cubs, born fifty to fifty-five days after conception. Both parents take care of the cubs, which are weaned when they are about a month old. At five months old mama and papa have done their share and the cubs are shoved out to scrounge for themselves.

Judge Williams had the following to say about the fox:

> The songs, stories and folklore of the Germanic races of the Aryan family contain many references to the fox. It seems to have been one of their more prominent animals. Another branch of the Aryan peoples, the Greeks, gave us the immortal classic "Aesop's Fables," in which the fox plays a major character. All of this indicates that the fox was well known to these people and probably lived uncomfortably close to the people who relied largely upon semi-domesti-

cated fowls and flocks of sheep and goats, for their living. But if the animal's fame depended upon the stories and songs of the people of Pecos County, the world would be short a great deal of vulpine literature.

The fox we find in America is the red fox, which is considerably different from the European animal that is so conspicuous in the nursery tales of our Anglo-Saxon forebears. If we may believe those same tales, and use a polite phrase, where we might use a very impolite one, it also possesses much less animal diplomacy than its European cousin. We do not have the fox in sufficient numbers to even make it a pest. If it has killed a lamb, or raided a poultry house in Pecos County during the time I have been here, I have not heard of it. As a pest to domestic animals, large or small, it cannot be compared to the panther, lobo, coyote and lynx.

I disagree with my father's assumption that foxes do not deprecate on lambs or poultry houses in this region. When my Angora goats were kidding, about twenty miles northeast of Fort Stockton, I was fairly certain the foxes were not only eating the afterbirth, but were also eating the small helpless kids.

Another time I owned some frying-size chickens, and one night I heard squawks of consternation coming from the chicken house. I charged outside to find a fox which had taken possession of one of my chickens and was chewing on it, right there in the yard. Both of these incidents occurred during the great depression of the 1930s, when money was scarce and food very dear — too dear to feed to a fox.

Judge Williams' article continues:

> Though many animals are included in the folklore stories among the Mexican people, the fox is not one of them. They call it "Zorra," and I do not know the origin of that name. It was taken from Spain, but I suspect the derivation is Moorish or Arabic like our names, "alfalfa, algaroba," etc. Unlike so many

Spanish names, it is not derived from Latin or Greek. The Goths once occupied Spain and planted a few of their names in the language, but their name for fox was the ancestor of our name for the animal, "fauhs." This is also the origin of the German name "fuchs." As the Moors were the only other race who imposed a strong influence on the Spanish language, I am left to suspect that "Zorra" is their gift.

Our Pecos County fox lives in or near the hills and makes its home in caves. Traces of it may often be found around rocky ledges. I have never seen it in the lowlands of the county, and if it ever dwelled there and burrowed out its den in the earth as the coyote now does it has not been brought to my attention. It feeds largely upon the native fruits. Like many animals and insects, the fox is partial to the pitahaya. When the pitahaya ripens, signs of the fox may be found abundantly scattered on the rocky ledges where the plant grows. It is no slight task for a nimble-fingered man to extricate the pitahaya from its resting place where it is barricaded by the long and ardent thorns peculiar to that cactus. It would be interesting to discover what proverbial animal cunning the fox uses to secure the fruit without getting severely speared by the thorns. Evidently these "grapes" do not hang too high for Mr. Fox.

Many of our urban residents are unaware of one local fruit which the fox considers delicious. I allude to the Texas persimmon which grows in the talus at the foot of rocky ledges all over the southern part of the county. The fox probably gets most of this fruit after it has dropped to the ground, but it could reach the food before it drops on these low shrubs. The persimmon is a relatively small shrub, distinguished by its glossy green leaves. The fruit ripens from August to November.

Persimmons and other fruits and seeds nourish the fox throughout the summer and fall seasons. The cold winter and the long dry spring are the seasons when our friend Reynard finds it most difficult to eke out a living. During this strenuous period of time, the fox has the companionship, but not the sympathy of the entire animal world. The fruit-bearing plants are barren, most of the birds have migrated, lizards and insects are dormant in their hiding places, and Mother Earth presents a cold, cheerless face to her tenants who are seeking daily bread. Hunger and cold weather press the poor little fox into sore straits. It becomes not only the hunter but the hunted. The famished lobo, panther and coyote, haunted by the spectre of starvation, faces Mr. Fox; the larger, stronger animals are pursuing him with desperate tenacity, and he sometimes has difficulty escaping some companion of the wild who is convinced Reynard would look good on the menu.

During the difficult seasons the capacity of a country to maintain life is sorely tested. The strength of a timber is measured by its weakest spot. By the same token, our dry springs, the weakest season of the year — measures the capacity of our area to sustain animal life of all types — domestic as well as wild. During the summer, fall and early winter we can graze twice as many numerical limit of our herds and flocks. We set the bounds beyond which we cannot safely pass when the earth lies parched and sere for week after week and month after month during the early spring.

During this time of famine, our resourceful friend, the fox, resorts to chasing the birds that have not migrated to fairer fields. He digs in the ground after the larvae of many insects which lie dormant. He turns over or scratches under rocks, finding an occasional lizard, asleep in its winter home. On sunny days it hangs around prairie dog holes hoping to catch a marmot out for a little fresh air and sunshine. The fox also likes a strange fruit which is still ripe and growing long after ordinary seeds and fruits have gone to sleep in the bosom of the earth. This is the fruit of the "tasajillo," a name with a most strange and interesting history.

In "The Honca Accursed," written by O. W. Williams around 1903, the Judge describes the tasajillo plant thusly: "Over there is the tasajillo, an Italian brave, hiding under cover at the street corner, eager to thrust his stiletto into his unsuspecting victim, ready as he does so to draw back into obscurity." Williams continues his present article on the tasajillo and the fox:

> This is the fruit a cereus of the cactus family. I think there is only one variety of this plant in Pecos County, although I have found two varieties in the Big Bend country. This shrub throws up a cluster of slender branches, lined from top to bottom with rows of keen, sharp thorns. The thorn is long and slender and enters the skin very easily and without much provocation, but any cowboy can testify to its reluctance to come out. In November and December, a bright red berry about the size of a gooseberry ripens between these thorns. Evidently the skin of this berry is very resistant to the evaporative power of the sun and wind, for unless it is picked, the berry remains on the plant until late the following spring without showing much shrinkage. During lean times, our so-called "blue" quail has nothing to eat but these berries. I have often killed them when there was nothing in their crops but the half-digested remains of these berries. The fox resorts to eating this same berry in times of dire hardship. Apparently he exhibits the same skill in getting the fruit without being stuck by the thorn that he shows in getting the pitahaya.
>
> It came as quite a surprise to me to discover that the fox relished wheat as a food in this country. I recalled the biblical story of Samson using the foxes to fire the wheat fields of the Philistines — for the foxes were proving almost as destructive to that wheat as if they had carried fire into it, as Samson's pets did. Since almost no wheat is now raised in this county, the resident reader will wonder, not where I saw the foxes — but where I saw the wheat. I shall have to go back to some ancient history to explain.
>
> In the year 1887, I was engaged in classifying state school lands along the Rio Grande River between Presidio del Norte and El Paso. Leaving Presidio I rode up the river on the north side some 25 miles

until I came to a small Mexican settlement called "Ruidosa." A ditch had been cut out of the River and carried along the low first bottom of the river on the north side for several miles, leaving between the ditch and river a fringe of rich bottom land from 100 yards to half a mile in width. Cottonwoods which were apparently 10 or 15 years old were growing on the ditch. The entire fringe of bottom land was sowed in wheat and at the time I was there the wheat was passing from the "milk" to the "dough" stage. Near the head of the ditch George H. Brooks, an "old timer," operated a small flour mill run by water power.

The road was near the ditch and ran adjacent to it, and as I rode along my attention was arrested by the sight of two men vigorously throwing clubs at some animal in the fork of a large cottonwood tree.

On the ground below two or three dogs frantically yelped encouragement to the men. Eventually the animal was dislodged, and the dogs killed it. My curiosity drew me over to the carcass, and I discovered it was a fox. The Mexicans told me that they must keep constant watch because of foxes depredating on their wheat. I spent the night with Samuel J. Hensley who ran a small store in the village, and I saw approximately 100 fox skins piled up behind the counter. Mr. Hensley said when the wheat went into the "milk" stage, the foxes swarmed down from the hills and did a great deal of damage. During this stage of their wheat crops, the Mexican farmers had to stand guard night and day to protect their crops.

In Fort Stockton, our Mexican farmers must guard the Indian corn when it reaches the "milk" stage — this time the villain is the crow. One night in 1880, I camped in the Tixeras Canyon in New Mexico near a small ranch owned by a man named Carpenter — called "Don Carpenterio" by the Mexicans. Mexican tenants had planted the land in corn. During the night I was aroused by a great uproar. I heard several shots from the direction of the ranch, and could see numerous pine knot torches weaving about in various spots. Those were the days when the savage Apache chief, Victoria, was tracing a path of blood throughout the country — so we armed ourselves hastily, and hurried over to the ranch to see what the commotion was all about.

We found that the corn was in the milk stage and the people were standing guard to protect their crop from bears. Nevertheless, some bears had sneaked into the corn and wrecked some damage. Needless to say, no bears were killed, for as one elderly Mexican remarked to me — they were not hunting bears, they were protecting corn. My assertion that killing a raiding bear was protecting corn, was received with good-natured contempt.

Since most of my life was lived in towns or small settlements, I never had much experience with foxes. However, one night Ernest Riggs, Pete Hill and I were following the hounds in our pasture seven miles west of Fort Stockton. Our dogs were hot on a trail and soon bayed. When we reached them, they were holding a small gray fox about eight or ten feet high up in a mesquite tree.

The six feet, five inch Pete had no difficulty in reaching up and violently shaking the fox off the limb. When it dropped abruptly among the dogs, they were completely surprised and dumbfounded. The fox probably also used his exterior glands to neutralize the sensitive noses of the hounds. He wasted no time, and raced out from under their legs and scrambled for freedom. The hounds didn't even attempt to pick up its trail.

I understand that most foxes which are seen today are red in color. The Judge indicated that most of them which were seen between 1884 and 1908 were all red foxes.

Charlie Stone said:

"A fox will get rabies, then they all get it and soon they all die. They call it distemper but it's not. One day on the Dean's ranch [Reeves County] a man named Hauffman had some ducks and chickens. This fox was chasing the ducks and chickens and even Hauffman. So he [Hauffman] went up a windmill. I saw this and got a pole and killed him [the fox]. He wasn't foaming at the mouth but he was weak and thin and too slow to bite anything."

The fox has played a prominent role in our nursery rhymes and bedtime stories for children. If we depend on our idioms we consider him quite a clever fellow. We speak of people being "quick as a fox," "sly as a fox," and "dumb like a fox." The last expression means someone is merely "playing dumb," while in reality they are quite intelligent. We also speak of a man as being a "foxy fellow," meaning that he's hard to pin down to a definite answer or opinion.

Our own red fox is considered innocuous and at most is normally a pest rather than a depredator — unless you are a chicken or wheat farmer.

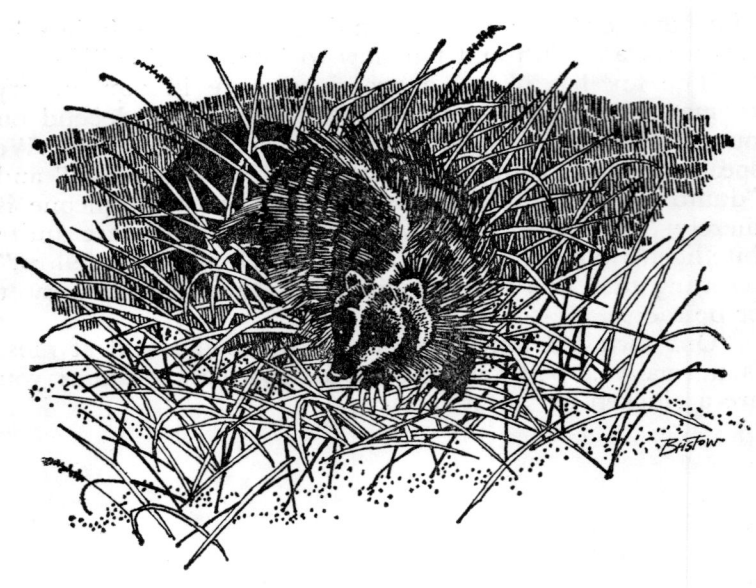

The American Badger
(Taxidea Taxus)

Badgers in North America live from southwestern Canada and the north-central part of the United States to Central Mexico. I have seen them in Oregon and Texas.

They grow only about two feet long and reach ten or twelve inches in height, but the little beasts are totally fearless. They are equipped with dangerous inch-long claws for digging and/or fighting. With the exception of its stomach, the badger's body is covered with long, thick hair which acts somewhat like a coat of armor. To a very large extent, the density of this fur protects the badger from the effect of bites from his assailants. His fur is a mixture of gray and yellowish brown, becoming a lighter red and gray shade around the belly. A white stripe travels from its nose, over the head, and down the middle of the back toward its short stubby tail.

The badger burrows its living quarters and usually breeds sometime in August. In the late spring, the female badger snuggles into her home and gives birth to a litter of about five. Within a week the eyes of the cubs are open, and within one month, when they reach about the size of a rabbit, they are weaned.

Reportedly, the sow is not tolerant of refuse in her home and is supposed to dig holes outside the den for latrines. I doubt that they dig separate holes, but from the looks of most badger dens, they do go outside to relieve themselves.

Although it will eat any animal it can catch, it also eats vegetation. It is supposed to be the greatest of diggers and invades the holes of gophers and prairie dogs, traveling by night from one burrow to another, devouring the hapless occupants. I have seen little evidence of its success in digging out gophers. That is understandable, for gophers dig long, endless passageways with a surface hole every now and then for them to come up. Even if the badger dug down a foot and one-half to two feet, reaching the large passageway of the gopher, he would still have from two hundred yards to miles to dig before cornering his quarry.

Judge Williams expounds on the badger:

> The homely and awkward badger belongs to a family designated by the imposing title of "The Plantigrades." In its Latin form, this is a rather aristocratic patronymic. Like the family name of some of the Italian counts and dukes, it loses some of its aristocratic flavor when translated into plain Anglo-Saxon. Its literal meaning is "those who walk on the sole of the foot." If you have ever compared the track

of a bear to that of a cat or dog, you can better appreciate the appropriateness of this surname.

Let me illustrate this difference by supposing a human being to crawl or travel on all fours. If he places the weight of his body in moving or standing upon his fingers and toes alone, then he would move and stand as the cat and dog do. If it became the customary mode of locomotion of the human family then in time the palm of the hand would become part of the forearm, while the sole of the foot would similarly become a part of the leg, and at the same time, the fingers and toes would develop pads as in the dog and cat.

On the other hand, suppose he could and did, place the palms of his hands and the soles of his feet flatly and squarely on the ground. In that case he would be walking, as the bear, the coon, the skunk and the badger walk, on his palms and soles. He would then be a "plantigrade," as opposed to cats and dogs, which walk on what we may call their fingers, and further as opposed to the cow which walks on two fingers, and the horse which goes on one. The striking resemblance of a bear's track to a human footprint has often occurred to those who have examined them.

If you will stroll along the banks of Comanche Creek after a rain, you may spot the broad, oval track of the palm of a coon on the bare ground — with the faint marks left by the slender, elongated fingers. [During the Judge's day, you could follow this suggestion. However, this stream has failed to run for a number of years because of pumping water for irrigation.] Cross our high plains in the dryest drouth and you may see what you believe to be the tracks of the same animal. But scrutinize more carefully — though the difference is slight, what you are looking at is the "spoor" of a badger. Though the coon and the badger belong to the same family and are near the same size, many of their habits and customs are very different.

The coon must live near water, therefore, he is limited to a narrow field of existence. Like a slender thread, his life lies up and down the length of a creek. He subsists solely upon the animal marshes. The badger is at home all over the Trans-Pecos and is specially adapted to the dryer parts. The desultory, uncertain rainfall in this semi-arid country apparently satisfies his need for water. He feeds upon animal life and is not a vegetarian.

The habits of its victims compel the badger to literally scratch for its existence every day. Mr. Badger is not an agile or swift animal, but the food he selects is not sluggish or inactive prey. He has little cunning and is not deceptive. His only sure and efficient means of making a living lie in his powerful claws and legs. On the surface of the earth, he would be unable to chase and catch gophers, prairie dogs and other marmots, but thanks to those powerful claws and legs, he can pursue and catch them under the ground. His whole life is one of leisure above ground and toil beneath the surface. He has scattered the monuments of his labor throughout this area. Many a cowboy bears a grudge against this harmless and rather beneficial animal. Sometime or other, while in headlong flight after a refractory cow or horse his steed had unwarily stepped into a badger hole. The least that can happen is that horse and rider come to earth — abruptly — often they come to grief. Cowboys generally attempt to shoot or lasso the badger.

I go a little further, to recite that many cowboys were killed or seriously injured when their speeding mount stepped into a badger hole. I saw one cowboy lying on his deathbed in his room in the Riggs Hotel after just such an accident. His horse had fallen on him. I can still envision that young man barely breathing through his mouth and nose because some of his insides had been pushed up into those organs.

As a small boy on the range, I was advised by seasoned cowboys to always ride my horse on the run with a tight rein. The supposition was that if the horse fell under those conditions, its head would throw the rider off ahead of it so that the boy or man would not be caught under the body of the horse. One day I was looking back when my horse stepped in a badger hole. I was still looking back when I hit the ground, and crawling forward, I saw the horse turn a flip and land in back of me.

The Judge continues on the subject of the badger:

> Yet it is really a benefit to the range on which it lives. This point was made clear to me many years ago by Mr. S. A. Purinton, who told me that he made it a rule on his ranch that badgers should not be killed. [The Purinton ranch was about forty-five miles south of Fort Stockton.] The animal feeds on prairie dogs, and one might say that the increase of badgers means less prairie dogs. These marmots live upon grass and grass roots, and the effect of any extraordinary increase in their numbers would be unusual destruction of grass. Now the fecundity of the prairie dog is great, probably giving it rank, in that respect, with the cottontail rabbit. If left without effective checks upon its increase, it would soon multiply and destroy great ranges of grass, as we are told the English rabbit has done in Australia.
>
> The prairie dog is beset by an army of foes. Birds swoop upon it from the air; animals stalk it above ground; and reptiles, badgers and skunks pursue it beneath the ground. Despite the great loss resulting from the combined efforts of these "captains of industry," the poor fleeced victim has managed to increase in population in Pecos County in the last 20 years. This increase is evidenced by the larger scope of country devastated by the formation of new prairie dog towns and colonies. In the course of a few years, the animal utterly destroys most varieties of grass around its home. Possibly one or two varieties may be able to survive its onslaught, yet they are cropped so closely that their value for grazing purposes is decreased.
>
> This evidence indicates that extermination of the prairie dog should be the policy of our ranchers and settlers. They should also encourage the increase of any animal, reptile or bird which preys upon it — provided that animal, reptile or bird is not a dangerous pest in other respects. To some extent, the

coyote and lynx are slight pests; because it is a carrier of hydrophobia, the skunk is a decided pest; the poison of the rattlesnake decrees him a pest; but the badger and the owl are harmless in every way. [The Judge was unaware that the badger sometimes killed sheep.] The increase of the prairie dog is not difficult to understand when you consider that its natural enemies — the rattlesnake, and the skunk — are rapidly decreasing. The lynx is decreasing more slowly, while the coyote is certainly not increasing.

I consider it necessary to preserve the badger, hawk and owl, for the settlement of Pecos County will surely bring about a decrease in some of the prairie dog's potent enemies. There is no practical way to facilitate an increase of the badger, the hawk and the owl, but we can at least let them live and work without any disturbance on our part. Judging from experience over the past 25 years, we must do something more about the prairie dog. I suggest using poison and every other practical manner of extermination on prairie dogs, or livestock and poultry predators. Someday soon, we must unite in this purpose and act together. In the meantime do not kill out the badgers.

We have some expert diggers among our native animals, such as the skunk and the coyote. The coyote can excavate a home for itself in the ground. The pocket gopher has some secret method of digging from his underground "pipe-lines" up to the surface. He leaves his path full of dirt and yet it is passable to him. The prairie dog digs a hole according to some uniform rule laid down by some old patriarch way back in the early history of the family. He deflects only when some obstacle appears in his path. But none of these can equal the speed with which the badger cuts his way underground.

Many years ago I heard a story about a sheep herder who lived in this county. He had built a winter "dug-out" against the side of a hill. The smoothly cut face of the hill served as the back wall of his home. Late one evening he was relaxing at the entrance of his dug-out when a badger raced past him and sped inside his home. The surprised herder hurried in and lit his lamp to discover where the varmint had hidden. He was probably pleased to discover that the animal was furiously digging into the back wall of his dug-out. During the short span of time the herder consumed in lighting the lamp, the badger had succeeded in burying himself in the earth beyond the length of his body.

The badger uses its talent for digging to catch prey. The victim strives to burrow away from the pursuing badger — while the badger digs furiously toward its intended meal. The end is usually inevitably in the badger's favor unless the pursued can hide behind some obstacle which the bulky badger cannot pass.

Possibly the name "badger" originated from the ancient British, or at least from a Celtic source. It meant "a carrier of corn." English peasants raised a type of corn quite different from the Indian corn introduced from America. The English badger was noted for its habit of pilfering this corn and carrying it off to its burrows. The American badger is a different specie from the English, and has no such habit — at least not in the Trans-Pecos area, for we have no corn for it to pilfer.

All animals, even some which are now extinct, aided mankind in ways which are not readily discernible. Looking back through the dimness of space, we can see that for an aeon the earth was not a fit habitation for man. Perhaps unwittingly, the animal and vegetable world were mute John the Baptists, toiling in the wilderness to "make straight the way of the Lord." The effect remains the same, whether or not this was the result of a preordained plan, or simply the natural results of material forces striving to survive. A rich, fertile earth was prepared for the domicile of man.

In our semi-arid West, the badger and many other burrowing animals and insects play their simple part in preparing the soil for man's use. They constitute what we may term as "Nature's plow." It is common knowledge that sod land must be plowed and harrowed several times before it is in peak condition for culture. This stirring of the soil appears to be even more necessary in semi-arid areas than in humid regions. But the short time the farmer spends preparing his land for cultivation represents only a fraction of the total preparation the land has received.

The farmer is reaping the benefit of centuries of preparation when animals and plants tended the earth. Throughout long ages they plowed the land, turning it up to the warm sun, allowing the wind and rain to harrow it. Though we now consider some of them contemptible, without them the earth would have lain indurated, unaerated and destitute of the humus so essential to plant life. In humid areas the earthworm performs a lot of this labor. In more arid regions, other insects and animals replace the lowly but valuable earthworm. In our area the ant burrows out a community home; the termite plasters twigs with mud; and the grasshopper bores holes in which to deposit its eggs. Each of these insects constitutes a tiny plow. Lizards scratching out places of refuge under stones or bushes serve as somewhat larger plows.

Moving up Nature's ladder we find the larger animals that contribute to the work. In building their homes, coyotes and cottontail rabbits turn up the underground and sub-soils to the air and the sun. In this county the prairie dog and gopher plow a deeper furrow, as if in penance for the damage they do in other ways. The badger, with his unequalled ability to dig, devotes his whole life to the service of turning the earth. This work continues until the settler buries his plow and drives out the animals which have been tending the soil.

The activities of many animals and insects have such a complex and indirect influence on the interests of man that it is difficult to decide which ones are beneficial and which are detrimental. It is imperative that we use far-sighted judgement in making these decisions — and even then, only He who keeps the great Ledger of Existence can balance the account perfectly. We may venture to use our judgment when the account of some animal is manifestly one-sided. In our semi-arid region, I believe it is safe to conclude that the badger lies mainly on the credit side of our ledger.

No one can ride over the western United States without seeing some evidence of the badger. Our professional trapper, Charlie Stone, said:

> A badger will kill and eat a rattlesnake. They kill it by biting it through the head. They'll drag the snake across the country, maybe four or five miles. When you come along and see the trail you might think someone came by on a horse with a loose rope on him. The badger feeds the snake to the baby badgers.
> A badger will try to kill a sheep when it's bedded down and then cover it up with grass or brush and dig a hole under it in order to have food nearby.
> Once a rancher called me out and said I've got a cat killing my sheep. I said I'd be out there that evening. Well, I went out there and he told me where it was and I went out saw it was a badger that killed the sheep and dug a hole under the neck of the sheep and holed-up in there. The sheep had been bedded down when the badger got him by the neck.

Charlie also told me that he had trapped eight or ten badgers which had dragged the chains and traps to their holes and managed to get inside. When he followed the trail to the den it proved nearly impossible to pull the badger out. In fact, the feat could not be done by hand, and Charlie attached the chain to his pickup truck to retrieve his trap and the badger. He also said that on two or three occasions, he had pulled the badger's leg off, and the badger was still in the hole.

I have heard cowboys say that it was almost impossible to pull a badger out of his hole with a rope. They believed that the animal swelled and completely filled the hole.

To my knowledge there has been no concerted effort to exterminate the badger, yet the animal seems to have decreased in numbers since the Judge's day and time. Perhaps the mass poisoning of prairie dogs in the 1920s and '30s influenced that circumstance. However, the resourceful badger turned to feeding on rats, and one now notices less rat nests in this area today.

The Skunk

Called "stink kitty," "pole cat," plain old "varmint," and a few unprintable names — the skunk is not one of man's favorite animals. Relative to the skunk, in 1908, Judge Williams wrote the following:

> This animal belongs to the badger-like division of the family of weasels. It is only found in the New World, where it suffers an ill reputation. In Europe, it stands in still less repute. The first account of the skunk was given to Europeans by Sagard who described it as an "enfant de diable." The name is sometimes used as a synonym to denote a contemptible fellow and to express a feeling of profound disgust for an animal or human being.
>
> It is probable that our evil opinion of the animal

in this part of the world is almost exclusively due to two facts connected with it. First, there is the skunk's ability to emit an intensely penetrating and disagreeable odor. There is no other animal in the world which possesses equally the power to disseminate its odors through the air and even through fairly solid substances to such an extent as the yellowish liquid which the processes of nature have wrought out and secreted in the glands of this animal.

There are essences, such as sulphuretted hydrogen, which may diffuse a more powerful odor into a small space, but I think it may be safely asserted that no similar quantity of any extract or compound known to the pharmacopoeia can spread its odor to such a distance and in such power as is attained by this product of nature's skill. On several occasions in camp I have been rendered uneasy and suspicious, believing a skunk to be in close proximity because of the intensity of the odor. Later, I would find that it was more than half a mile away.

How persistent this odor is! It will remain in a spot for months. Indeed, those compelled to be neighbor to it will become so accustomed to it that only the stranger can detect it.

Some 30 years ago, before age and experience taught me to be wary of the animal, my attention was very disagreeably and very forcibly drawn to this peculiarity of the odor. I had engaged a party of surveyors for several months to work on the Staked Plains. One day a rain caught us in a prairie dog town. It was a heavy downpour, and the water came rushing down some small draws which ran through the dog town. Some enterprising spirits in the party got out mattocks and spades and proceeded to trench channels from these draws, and to carry the water to the dog holes. In this manner they caught quite a number of dogs. As the water rose in the hole, the prairie dog rose with it and was easily caught. The sport was infectious and I fell in with the party. I encountered a different varmint than I or any other member of the party had anticipated.

I had drowned out an unusually vigorous customer,

but he escaped me and took flight into a neighboring hole. I followed him, trenched water to his new hole, and, placing the blade of the spade over the hole so as to keep the dog in the water until it should be rendered sufficiently insensible, I waited for the proper time to lift up the spade and catch the dog. This practice had been successful, so one can imagine my surprise when I lifted my spade to find a full grown very unfriendly skunk instead of a half-drowned prairie dog. Mr. Skunk backed out very much bristled up, and advanced on me tail first. To make a long story short, I killed the skunk, but came out rather "disabled for action," as our naval reports sometimes say of certain ships.

This was bad enough, but the worst was yet to be realized. Our party had been in the field longer than we had originally intended and we had run short of supplies. Socks, shoes, pants, shirts and other clothes had either worn out or been discarded and no one had a garment in reserve. Most of us were scantily clad, so I could get no change of clothes. I became a sort of pariah among my people, as I could not eat in the general mess nor sleep on the common campground. With the passing of time I failed to notice the odor, but wherever I went the others respectfully gave way, so I knew it was still there. I tried the friendly suggestion of the Irish cook and slept at night with my clothes under dirt. I had washed and scrubbed with such soap as we had, but it all seemed to no avail. I used to lie awake at night studying various methods to get rid of my companion, the odor. I was somewhat sentimental in those days and disposed to quote Byron or Tom Moore, and I repeated often these lines:

"You may break, you may shatter the vase
   if you will,
But the scent of the roses will hang 'round
   it still."

If only this had been the scent of roses!

It took approximately three weeks to get to a

frontier store where I could get a change of clothing. From the disagreeable twitching of the merchant's nostrils as he sold me my outfit, I gathered that the scent of roses hung 'round me still.

Judging from what I have read, the odor of musk is the only thing which ranks with the odor of the skunk for endurance, and it is also a product drawn directly from Nature's alembic. I have read somewhere a statement that the odor of musk can be detected yet in some room occupied by Mary Stuart several hundred years ago. I am inclined to believe that the deer or deers which furnished that musk were born long after Mary Stuart's death. However, the fact that such a contention can be seriously made goes to show how general is the belief in the endurance of the odor of musk.

At one time it was believed that the inhalation of skunk musk was of great benefit in cases of asthma. If there was anything to this belief Pecos County could advantageously set up an Asthmatic Sanitarium down around the 7D Mountain. The rock crevices at its northeast point could be saturated with the odor and your asthmatic patients could live in comfort during the balance of their lives on its craggy edges. If the odor did not persist like Mary Stuart's musk, they could easily obtain a fresh installment when it faded away. While Pecos County may be short on some very interesting and valuable animals, it is not short on skunks.

Another reason for the evil name borne by the skunk in these localities is the fact that it carries with it the danger of a dread disease — hydrophobia. There is such a strange incredible circumstance about this fact, that for many years I refused to believe it — The animal is of the same species and variety here as those found in the Mississippi Valley and further east. No one in those countries entertains any idea of skunks carrying hydrophobia, nor have I ever heard of an authenticated case of the disease being communicated by the skunk anywhere east of the 100th meridian. No one knows why the circumstance exists, and dozens of questions arise in one's mind. Whatever the reason, why should skunks in Pecos County communicate hydrophobia, while they do not do so in Kentucky or New Jersey?

Now note another difference — In those countries east of us, such as Kentucky and New Jersey, the dog acts as the chief agent in carrying hydrophobia. On the contrary, in Pecos County during the last 25 years I cannot recall a single well authenticated case of a dog having hydrophobia. With one exception some three or four months ago, we have had no suspicions of hydrophobia in dogs. In this case I understand that no animals bit by the suspect were kept alive long enough to test the correctness of the suspicion. I saw the animal credited with the disease and was very skeptical about the correctness of the charge, though perhaps it was true.

Another thing which I consider unaccountable is this: Many persons in this county have received skunk bites. At least twelve or fifteen people who are now living and in good health assert this fact. Most of them were bit on the face, although a few received bites on their feet or hands. I have never heard of such occurrences in Kentucky or Missouri. Why should this difference exist? It cannot be explained by saying that people in Pecos County sleep much more exposed to the attacks of animals than people of older more settled countries. You have only to go back a few years to find the people of those older countries living under the same frontier conditions and under the same exposure to the animal as the people of this country now do. Yet pioneer memoirs report no such state of affairs. Old books relating to life in the Mississippi Valley when it was a frontier make no mention of special danger from skunks. There were mad dogs in those days and more than one tragic human death is recorded from communication of hydrophobia by a dog but not one that I can recall from the bite of a skunk.

I have heard of one case of a lynx with hydrophobia and one case of a coyote, and we have two deaths undoubtedly due to the communication of the disease by a skunk — but none from that of the dog.

At least that is the case so far as my recollection serves me. It would not be reasonable to draw any important conclusions from such a small basis, but it is a matter of common knowledge all over the extreme Western part of Texas — that of the deaths from hydrophobia, those resulting from skunk bite are the most numerous in this section. Let me recite those from our immediate neighborhood.

According to newspaper reports, a man named Simpson died at Marathon ten or more years ago from this disease. I cannot vouch for the truth, but rumor says that he had been bit by a skunk about eleven months prior to his death. I believe he was a middle-aged man.

Over five years ago poor Tom Valentine died in our town from the same cause and the facts were fairly well ascertained. He had been bit by a skunk while sleeping out in an old house or dug-out 35 miles south of Fort Stockton. The animal seized him by the lip and was torn loose with considerable difficulty. About 18 days afterwards the disease appeared in him, but was not diagnosed at once. Even if it had been recognized at once to be hydrophobia it would have been too late to use any remedies.

He died after suffering some days. This case was so well known that I presume there can be no doubt that this death was due to inoculation from skunk bite. Tom was about 20 years old.

Reportedly, Tom was tied in bed to prevent him from biting and infecting other people with rabies. Mrs. O. W. Williams, the Judge's wife, was among those good women who took turns nursing him and aiding the Valentine family. An hour or two before Tom died, he called for his mother and told her good-by for he realized he would die shortly.

Judge Williams continued:

The following is the only incident directly within my personal knowledge concerning a rabid skunk:

In 1890, I was building a canal on the Pecos River in the north part of the County. I was boarding with Mr. Goodin, and one evening at supper we heard the yelps of a small puppy which Mr. Goodin kept tied near the back door. Racing outside, we discovered it had been bit by something on its nose which was bleeding. We got a lantern and searched around the house, finding a skunk at one corner. The animal tried to get away, but we had it cornered. It fought until I killed it with a pitchfork. There was nothing unusual in its conduct — almost all other skunks I have killed have been willing to fight when pressed. I mention this because the puppy died in convulsions four or five days afterwards and Mr. Goodin pronounced it a case of hydrophobia.

It is possible that the animal [skunk] carries the germs of the disease, and yet is immune from the disease itself. I have never heard of anyone witnessing the skunk in convulsions or otherwise indicating that it had hydrophobia. In every other animal affected by rabies the symptoms of the disease are very marked. Dogs, lynxes, coyotes, cows, horses have all been observed with the disease thousands of times and its progress and symptoms are very marked and similar. It would seem reasonable to expect to find the same history of the disease in the skunk as in other animals. And it may be that it runs the same course, but has not been observed owing to the nocturnal habits and underground life of the animal.

Yet there are times when I am led to suspect that the relation of the animal to the disease is peculiar and exceptional. This exceptional relation seems to exist, as I have intimated before, in the semi-arid West. It may be a relation existing from remote time. Hydrophobia was known to the Greeks and Romans during the times of Aristotle and Pliny and may have been a disease introduced into America after its discovery by Europeans. It is a very well known fact that the diseases of Europe and America were not the same at the time of the discovery. For instance, measles and smallpox were diseases unknown to the Indians and were peculiarly fatal to them, just as yellow fever was unknown to Europeans and became peculiarly fatal to them. There were also some diseases common to both continents. Some authors are disposed to claim that hydrophobia is a disease which has been common to all parts of the earth from some period of great antiquity. They point to its existence in the Islands of the South Seas at the time of discovery by Europeans, and to its presence in all quarters of the globe as evidence of an original existence long before the European sailed the seas, and inflicted his diseases as well as his dominion upon the natives. If such claims are true then it may be that the Indian knew the relation between the disease and the animal long before he heard the legend of the Fair God.

Yet if the disease was introduced into this country by Europeans then it has probably spread because a mad dog or other mad animal communicated the disease to a skunk, and the skunk in turn inoculated its fellows. A house in which consumption has existed continues to spread the disease to new inmates. Perhaps the underground home of the skunk gives the rabies germ an exceptional opportunity to maintain its germs dormant and protected for long periods of time. If so, these dens and nests may have spread the disease from generation to generation of animals.

But this question arises: If such conditions exist here and bring about the resulting prevalence of the disease among the skunks of this section why don't these same conditions bring about the same results in other countries? Why should the skunk in Western Texas carry and communicate the disease when the same skunk in Kentucky and Tennessee does not seem to carry and communicate it? Surely mere climatic difference cannot directly bring about that result. If it is a factor, it must be an indirect and secondary one.

Since writing my last article in *The Pioneer*, an incident has occurred in Pecos County which draws attention to a question raised in that article, viz: How is one to determine whether a bite from the skunk is harmless or dangerous in any particular case. We have many well authenticated cases in this country where the bite has proved innocuous, and a few where it has been known to be fatal, or where circumstances have shown that it might have been so. Hence it becomes a question of greatest importance when a wound has been inflicted by the animal to determine what step to take. If it is determined by any reasonably certain means of conjecture that the animal is in a stage to communicate hydrophobia, then the victim should take the shortest and quickest route to the Pasteur Institute at Austin. However, there is great expense and loss of time involved in the trip, and if there were any fairly certain means at hand to determine that the wound is harmless then this might be avoided. Unless some means of determining the question with reasonable certainty is devised most of us will be disposed to take no chances when life is the stake.

This was the position taken by Mr. Tom Sanderson in the incident to which I have referred. His little boy was bit while sleeping on a bed out of doors between two older persons. Mr. Sanderson had heard the animal making some disturbance a short time before it attacked the boy. He searched for the skunk and found it, but it slipped away from him in the darkness only to return later and bite the little boy. There was nothing in the conduct of the animal to rouse any suspicion that it was unusually affected. However, after the bite it was of vital importance to know if the boy was in danger of hydrophobia. It was apparently impossible for him to weigh the chances in the present state of available knowledge of such matters, so he took the only really safe course under all circumstances and sent the boy to the Pasteur Institute at Austin for treatment there.

Had it been a dog bite Mr. Sanderson, in all probability, would have been able to decide promptly and with reasonable certainty the danger of infection. Although it is occasionally masked, the disease runs a fairly regular and distinctive course in that animal, and its symptoms are well known and recognized by the public. But how is one to form any judgement as to the presence of the disease in the skunk? The animal's habits are largely nocturnal so that the benefits of observation are denied to us. Further, speaking as laymen, we do not even know that the disease runs its course in the skunk as in other animals. In all my life on the frontier, I have never heard of evidence to show that the animal dies from the disease. It is a matter easily tested by experiment, and I take it that the experts in the Pasteur Institute have determined it, but if so, I have never seen any report from them. It might be of great practical benefit to those of us who live in a country infested with these hydrophobia-carrying animals to have the well marked history of the disease given to us as it is developed in them.

As I have intimated before, everything that I have heard concerning the animal indicates that it may carry the rabies germ yet be immune from it. There is this circumstance to countenance the idea: Due to its habits, the animal, as a species, would be in great danger of destruction in some localities if the disease was scattered among its members. One animal might spread the disease to all of its kind in that neighborhood and unless there was whole or partial immunity there would be no remaining skunks in that locality. Yet in this county there has been no noticeable epidemic observed among them. Nor has there been any unusual mortality at any time, whether before or after the deaths of Simpson and Valentine. There has been nothing to indicate that the disease is especially fatal to the skunk. Yet we know that a single mad dog running through a country may leave behind the seeds of an epidemic of hydrophobia were it not for the restraining and quarantining exercised by man with a most determined and rigid hand. There is no such restraint possible in the case of a mad skunk. It runs its course unmolested by man.

It is said that a coyote will make a dinner off of a skunk and I have heard more than one Mexican express a decided relish for its flesh. But with these exceptions, the animal is not an object of contention as food for any part of the animal world, except to that small and repulsive member, to which even the beauty and splendid mechanism of the human frame must at last become food. Even the buzzard rejects it. Hence the varmint's increase is not checked by the presence of a formidable enemy preying upon it. Unlike the prairie dog and cottontail rabbit, it is not fenced in with a ring of devouring enemies, but finds itself enjoying comparative freedom from dangers of that kind. From a feeling of repulsion, a sentiment which evidently exists only in these parts, it is destroyed by man. In some places it is trapped and hunted for the value of its hide, but here no pecuniary reason enters into its destruction. It is simply repulsive and sometimes destructive to poultry and eggs, and so it is killed wherever it is found.

Judge Williams' daughter, Ermine Williams Garnett, afterward wrote the following about her experience at the ranch house on the river:

> We had been unable to get screens for the windows or doors of the ranch house, and during the hot weather it was necessary to leave the doors and windows open to let the breeze through. We could not have a lamp lighted at night because it would attract mosquitoes and other insects into the house. Often, instead of lighting a lamp, we would light smudge pots so that the smoke would keep some of the insects away. We children didn't like the smoke from the smudge pots any more than the mosquitoes did, and if the weather was good, we would climb up onto the flat-topped roof of the house to sleep. If there was a breeze, we got it, of course, and we were seldom bothered by insects up there. Quite often Father would sleep on the roof with us and we would spend an enjoyable evening as Father told us the names of the various stars and constellations. Mother, however, preferred to remain in her own bed inside the house.
> One night when Father was away from home my brother Waldo and I were wakened by Mother's call. She told us to put on our shoes and come down, as some sort of animal had gotten into the house and Fido [the dog] had followed it on into the milk room. We dressed and went down the ladder to join Mother in the house. She had left her glasses on the mantel

when she retired and did not want to leave the bed until she had them on. We got her glasses for her and lighted a lamp. During this time Fido was growling and barking at something in the milk room.

When we got to the room with a light the situation was even worse than had been thought. Fido had cornered a skunk in the milk room, and on our bringing the light to the room, the skunk began his concentrated protest in the best skunk fashion. We were unable to coax him into leaving the room, so Mother sent Waldo for a pitchfork and a crowbar. While I held the lamp, Waldo pinned the skunk down with the pitchfork and Mother killed him with the crowbar.

To one who has never encountered a skunk at his worst, the description of Fido's encounter may seem tame, but after all these years, I vividly recall the terrible odor that permeated not only the milk room but the entire house. It was necessary for the door to the milk room to be closed, and for months the room was used only as storage for unused articles.

When Judge Williams was writing his articles on animals, I was about thirteen years of age. The Judge's home was one of the old officers' quarters of Fort Stockton. It was built with high ceilings to aid in keeping the house cool in the summertime. Despite that, nights were much cooler outside the house and I frequently got a bedding roll and slept on the back porch.

I was awakened one night by a continual chirping sound, and thought it was probably made by a bird. I had recently shot and killed what my father identified as a monkey-faced owl, sometimes called golden owl, which covers a large part of the Americas. It is better known as the barn owl and has tremendous and remarkable ears for detecting the sound of rodents among twigs and leaves. As the owl had been shot on the framework above our underground cistern, and the noise I heard was coming from that direction, I thought it might be another owl. Instead, close to the edge of the cistern I saw a strange sight.

A skunk was chattering away as he stepped forward and then backward — time after time. Perhaps he was performing a ritual in celebration of the demise of one of his few mortal enemies. The next morning I examined the location and found his tracks which confirmed what I thought might have been a dream.

A few mornings later my mother plugged the skunk's small entrance under the porch, and informed me that Mr. Skunk was outside and available for us to move him away from the house and dispose of him. No one familiar with the varmints will kill a skunk close to where he lives. We cautiously maneuvered the "stinker" by the north end of the house where I picked up a canoe paddle. The skunk slowly ambled ahead of us with its beautiful striped tail hoisted straight up at full mast — a cute, harmless-looking piece of fluff if you didn't know better.

About one hundred yards from the house I went into action, leaped in front of the skunk and hit it a deadly blow with the canoe paddle. The skunk had simultaneously mobilized his defenses. I didn't know that his defense fore and aft was ambidextrous. I thought that when I was in front of it I was safe from his amazingly accurate aim with that potent weapon located on his rear end. Even today it's hard to realize my frontal attack failed so totally — but I was outclassed. The ruthless stink kitty had built-in equipment — two scent glands at the base of its tail, with a nozzle and accompanying muscular attachment, and with a graceful "swish" he fixed me good! He had made all of the calculations for my movement, and allowed for windage on the yellow charge and the atmospheric conditions on a moving target about four feet distant.

Despite the fact that the skunk is credited with doing the farmer a service by destroying larvae, field mice and other things which devour and destroy crops on the farmer's land, its actions are often in conflict with the farmer's interest, sometimes very disturbing.

Fifteen or twenty years later, Judge Williams' married

daughter, Mrs. Charles H. Garnett, and her three children were living on an irrigated farm about three miles north of Fort Stockton. At that time, if anyone in this vicinity had chickens they had to raise them. Eggs had to be hatched by the hen and thereafter both hen and chicks were kept in a chicken coop to protect them from varmints. Later they could be released to scratch for themselves and roost in the chicken house.

A skunk had made its home under Mrs. Garnett's house. Spotting it early one morning, she got her shotgun, drew a bead on the varmint and fired. Unfortunately the skunk moved when the gun discharged and Mrs. Garnett inadvertently killed her only rooster. It was Sunday, and the family normally drove into Sunday school and church. Instead, they had to pluck the rooster, dress, cook and eat him, and the contrary skunk was still a problem.

Mrs. Garnett's children thought they could do a better job at getting rid of the pest. Williams K., the son, had a trap and some experience with animals as he had trapped varmints to sell their fur. A trap was set and staked out just far enough away from the building where the children thought the skunk would be unable to get back under the house. The animal was caught. Immediately the house and region was contaminated with its foul, defensive-offensive odor and the little beast inched back under the house at the end of the chain attached to the trap.

After a hurried council of war, the kids decided upon an elaborate plan: one would grab the trap chain and jerk the skunk from under the house; another would slap a board over the varmint's entrance; and the third would hit the skunk on the head with a baseball bat as soon as it was safely pulled out. Battle plans were laid, but alas! This operation went astray. During the excitement while the uncooperative skunk was being pulled out from under the house, the youth with the baseball bat lost his coordination, footing or something, and crowned one of the other children on the head with the bat.

In addition to the nuisance a skunk contributes by simply being in the vicinity, there is the constant fear that one might be a carrier of hydrophobia as Judge Williams has stressed in his writing.

The *World Book* gives the following information on rabies:

> Rabies, or hydrophobia is an infectious disease that destroys the nerve cells of part of the brain and causes death. Human beings and most warm-blooded animals can get the disease. *Rabies* is a Latin word, meaning rage or fury. It probably received its name because infected animals often become excited and attack any object or animal in their way. Because one of the symptoms of rabies is an inability to swallow water, the disease often is called hydrophobia, which means fear of water.
>
> Rabies is caused by a virus that lives in the saliva of a host (carrier). Most mammals can carry the rabies virus. If the host bites another animal or a human being, or if some of its saliva enters an open wound, the victim may get rabies. Men and animals have also developed rabies after breathing the air in caves that contained millions of bats. The virus can enter mucous membranes, such as those lining the nose, but it cannot invade unbroken skin. Dogs and wild animals are the most common source of infection for human beings.
>
> When the virus enters the body, it travels along nerves to the spine and brain, producing inflammation. Once symptoms appear, death is inevitable. The symptoms develop about ten days to seven months after exposure.
>
> Symptoms in man — Among the first symptoms are pain, burning, or numbness at the site of infection. The victim complains of headaches and is unable to sleep. Muscle spasms make the throat feel full, and swallowing becomes difficult. Sometimes, the sight of water creates such painful throat contractions that drinking is dreaded. Later, the patient may have convulsions. But after a day or two, he lapses into a quiet

period, which progresses to unconsciousness and, finally, death. The disease lasts from two to twelve days.

Symptoms in dogs — The disease follows the same pattern as in man. During the period of excitation, the dog may wander great distances. It is aggressive, growling and barking almost constantly, and will attack without reason. From this stage the disease usually progresses to general paralysis, then death. Some rabid dogs never show signs of the excitative phase but only of the paralysis. This form of disease is sometimes called dumb rabies. Paralysis of the jaw and throat muscles are characteristic of this type of rabies.

Treatment — The most important treatment is to prevent the disease by vaccinating all dogs. A person bitten by any animal should immediately wash the area thoroughly with soap and water. The animal should be penned up and watched by a qualified person for symptoms of rabies. If these develop, the doctor begins to vaccinate the victim at once. He gives injections of vaccine daily for fourteen days or longer. If the animal cannot be found, the physician gives the injections to the victim as a safety measure.

Douglas Adams, a native of Fort Stockton, Texas, relates his unfortunate experience resulting from cutting off the head of a skunk.

I was working for the late Sid Slaughter, in charge of his large spread of 125 sections of land and 25,000 sheep on San Francisco Creek about twenty-five or thirty miles south of Longfellow. He had lots of Mexicans working. They were conveniently camped out all over the ranch. One cold, misty night in November while one of these Mexicans was squatting with his hands behind him and his back to the fire, a pole cat came up behind him and bit him through the finger. He killed it and later told me about it.

While cutting its head off to send it for determination of rabies I accidentally cut my finger and got the skunk blood on the cut. I took the head to Sanderson, packed it in ice and put in on the midnight train, addressed to Austin. Two or three days after returning to the ranch, Sid Slaughter came down and brought a telegram which stated that the pole cat had hydrophobia and advised us to start treatment on the Mexican within seventy-two hours. The seventy-two hours were almost up then, because the telegram had been in Sanderson a day or so before Sid came along. I didn't know then that I was supposed to take the treatment.

When I told the doctor about the cut on my finger, he said that I also would have to take the treatment. I got my Mexican and went to Sanderson. He happened to be a "wet" Mexican, who had illegally crossed the Rio Grande (supposedly got "wet" wading across the river), and was wanted by the United States immigration officers. We got there about twelve o'clock at night. I didn't want my Mexican to be picked up as an alien, nor did I want to be picked up for hauling him around. So I contacted members of the Border Patrol. They said, "We won't have anything to do with him; he's yours."

There wasn't any of the hydrophobia vaccine in Sanderson, so I went to Fort Stockton and there was none there or at Alpine. So Dr. Oswalt of Fort Stockton telephoned for some to be sent out and it arrived by plane on the next morning.

Afraid he would run off, we kept the Mexican in a jail in Fort Stockton while we were taking the shots. We took one shot every day for seven days. These shots were injected deep into the stomach by a hypodermic needle, two inches long. The shot was contained in a three- or four-inch cylinder as wide as one's thumb. The shot was extremely painful, and would burn three or four minutes after the shot was taken. Unfortunately, the injection needle was large and also hurt when pushed straight into the stomach. The first shot was the most painful of the seven because the doctor had me stand up with my back against the wall so I couldn't get away, and shoved the needle in. Afterward the shots were given to me by the nurse, who would pinch up the skin. That didn't hurt as much. The last day we took our shots I went to pick up the Mexican from the doctor's office and the Immigration officers had picked him up after we had gone through the trouble and expense of protecting him.

Prior to the creation of Pasteur's antidote for rabies in 1882 and for some time afterward the term *madstone* was applied to some kind of a stone which was supposed to be placed on the infected spot in an attempt to draw out the poisonous substance. This stone was a porous rock from the stomach of a white or albino deer. It drew the hydrophobia poison out of the flesh. Other sources identified the magic stone as a kidney or gallstone. The late J. Frank Dobie in his article of April, 1960, in the *Frontier Times,* wrote that "the stone was first moistened in milk — water would not be trusted — and applied to the wound. If the stone did not adhere, the person being treated was presumed not to have the virus. To do any good it had to stick to the flesh for a long time, drawing the poison out of the wound and absorbing it. . . ."

Whether bit by a skunk or dog under conditions which might indicate that the animal was mad, one could not take a chance that he was immune to the disease. Most people wanted the benefit of a madstone in the days before the antidote for rabies. Some preferred the stone even after the perfection of the antidote.

I was told of one incident concerning a cowboy named Teburcio Calderon. He was working on the Baldridge ranch north of Fort Stockton when he was bit by a skunk. A day or so after the bite he got sick and was frightened of the consequences of the bite. His comrades persuaded him to ride to Monahans and take the Texas and Pacific train to Toyah where he could be treated with a madstone. This he did and had no further trouble on account of the bite.

In another instance I have been told of a dog bite after which a man used a madstone. Regardless, the victim died within a few days.

It is said that nothing in this world is all good — and nothing is all bad. This applies even to a varmint like the skunk. Judge Williams has this to say:

> In many ways the animal is very serviceable to our race. It is the most inveterate destroyer of our insect enemies. For example, in this area we have a beetle known as the June Bug, which is quite harmful to our fruit, particularly to the ripening peach. This beetle lays its eggs about an inch underground, usually in ground covered with a sort of mulch of straw or manure. It is found in great abundance around old cattle or sheep corrals. The eggs lie dormant through the winter and the long dry spring, then hatch after the first rain into a worm known to us as the grub worm. This worm lies underground for some time, gradually growing and ripening from a chrysalis into the beetle. In this stage it is a favorite food for the skunk, and the animal at this time devotes its whole existence to the business of scratching up and eating these "grubs." It must detect the presence of the worm underground by its power of scent, and that sense must be acute. In all the holes scratched out by the animal in its search for grubs, you will always find that it went straight down to the grub as unerringly and undeviatingly as a bullet goes to the mark. There is no change of direction in the hole from top to bottom. During certain seasons of the year thousands of these little holes can be found in old sheep corrals, or about old manure beds and you can easily test this statement by examining them in May and June of each year.

Skunks also eat crickets, bugs, cutworms, other larvae and many insects which feed on plants. Hens' eggs, young chickens, birds and bird eggs are their favorite food. Mice in their shallow ground holes are easily dug out and eaten by the skunk.

Judge Williams went on to say:

> The June Bug is not alone on the menu of our

skunk. Every other insect is its lawful prey. Various kinds of grasshoppers, locusts, spiders and wasps all wind up in its greedy little jaws. In this manner its services are of value to us, as these insects are generally destructive to the plants cultivated by us. If they were not kept in bounds it would be impossible to cultivate the earth. Birds are of great help to us in destroying insects after they are on the wing, but the skunk is working at their destruction long before this stage, while they are still in the earth before they are transformed into insects.

Without the aid of bird and beast, insects would multiply in this country to such an extent they would be a curse to us. There would be nothing to check their increase save lack of food. After eating off our grasses and stripping our herbs and shrubs of leaves and bark they would die out, or would migrate to another country to lay waste the face of the earth. Our country would not only become desolate and useless to us, but would become a breeding ground for plagues which would periodically devastate other countries. Around 30 or 40 years ago nature's delicate balance was evidently upset, and devastating hordes of locusts descended on Kansas, Indian Territory and Texas and blighted the face of the earth. They swooped in from the great unsettled semi-arid country in the West. They had the same effect as some of the more famous Indian attacks — they temporarily halted advancing civilization. But like those attacks, the effect was only temporary, and in time the march of civilization was again ordered, regulated and planting outposts deeper and more firmly into the desert west.

Settlement and cultivation in the arid West is not well ordered in all respects. In many ways it acts blindly and by the brute force of material power. The first foes faced by man are first crushed, regardless of the ulterior effect. It is this which causes many reacting hardships upon the frontiersman. When the skunk and the coyote and the wildcat and rattlesnake are killed, it is because they are the most apparent enemies of

177

mankind. They are not necessarily, however, his most potent enemies. They have been playing their part in creating and maintaining Nature's balance between the animal and vegetable world of this uninhabited country. When they are removed this balance is disturbed. The pendulum then swings out of plumb.

The animals and insects which they have been keeping within bounds then increase enormously. In turn these increased numbers of animals and insects tend to put a strain on the vegetable world. This strain is then passed on to other plants and animals and the chain reaction continues indefinitely until it is almost impossible to calculate the ultimate results. It may be a hundred years before some of these results become apparent. It has required countless centuries for nature's forces to evolve into the harmonious balance which now exists and certainly one cannot expect a ruthless interference with that harmony to be measured by the rule at the time. But it is apparent that the interference must come, in fact is coming now, and we should at least exercise what judgement we can in making the disturbance as small as possible.

The first settlers are those upon whom the responsibility for the exercise of this judgement must largely fall. It is we who are first on the land who practically decide what animals and insects we shall first exterminate. And we face and fight what is most apparently an evil. In this we may, and probably will, act in some ways much to our own detriment. We have not made a study of the interacting powers of nature. We have much to do merely to survive, and we have no time for such studies. From the results of our hardships and exposures we contribute to maintain a Department at Washington which is especially devoted to such studies.

The Judge followed with many suggestions as to what the U.S. departments should do about the wildlife and insects in the United States, much of which has been done in the last seventy-two years.

To finish this chapter in a less distasteful manner please say rapidly and get your friends to say the following:

> The Skunk sat on a stump.
> The stump said the skunk stunk,
> and, the skunk said the stump stunk.

So the skunk and the stump make a real tongue twister!

The Jackrabbit and Cottontail

Scientists tell us that the jackrabbit is not a member of the rabbit family, but is a hare. There are two kinds of that type hare in North America: the white-tailed and the black-tailed.

The white-tailed jackrabbits (Lepus townsendi) inhabit the American Northwest and British Columbia and change their coat from a summer buff to a winter white. They are somewhat similar in size, habits, and other characteristics to our black-tailed jackrabbit (Lepus californicus) of the Southwest. The latter has enormous, long, broad ears, and a tail longer than a rabbit's. The enormous ears are responsible for the contracted name, jackrabbit; this contraction is derived from jackass rabbit.

Recalling the jackrabbit's original name always reminds me of a conversation I overheard in 1915 on a train between Alpine and Marfa, Texas. I was seated with some Mennonites, two women and a man, who were strangers to the Southwest. Their home was in northeast Canada. The man, apparently better informed than the women, was acting as tour guide. He was explaining that this part of Texas was noted for being a great cattle country. Yet, throughout the day, as the train moved west, he hadn't seen a single cow. One woman asked, "What else is this country noted for?"

He replied, "The jackrabbit, because it is a lot larger than our rabbits, and has great big ears."

About that time the train pulled into Marfa, Texas, where a few burros were standing around. "Oh!" cried the woman. "Look at those big jackrabbits!"

Our West Texas jackrabbit ranges from Oregon to Nebraska, and south into Mexico. With its buff brown, or gray coat, huge, drooping ears and black-tipped tail, this species is unmistakable. It matures to a length of twenty-eight inches or more. The prolific jackrabbit female has a litter of seven or eight babies several times a year. The young ones quickly become independent, and we would rapidly have a jackrabbit population explosion if so many predatory animals didn't consider them to be gourmet meals. Even so, West Texas farmers and ranchers frequently have "rabbit drives" to rid the vicinity of the furry little imps.

Russell Payne, a former ranchman of Fort Stockton, has ridden over much of the Trans-Pecos range and has seen many jackrabbits which were not grown and some while they were still in the nest. "The nest," he said, "is dug out under a bush much in the shape of a hen's nest, sometimes with some straw or leaves on its bottom and sides. In the hill country, where the sacahuista bush [Nolina erumpens] grows, the jackrabbit prefers to make its nest hidden beneath that plant's leaves. North of the Fort Stockton region, most any kind of bush will do."

I asked Russell why the jackrabbit still existed as a species if its young were so vulnerable to all its enemies. He said, "Although the young are greatly exposed, the female litters several times a year."

Some sixty-five years ago, Judge Williams had gathered considerable information on the jackrabbit and wrote the following:

> Now we look on this scene of animal life after a destructive change. The buffalo has been utterly destroyed from its old range. The antelope still retains a feeble foothold in isolated parts of its former home, and a somewhat stronger one in what was once an adjunct territory, the high plateaus ringed in by the mountains, but will soon be extinct. The coyote has kept its suzerainty better, but the prospect of the conversion of the plains into farms spells the eventual extinction of this denizen. It might have existed indefinitely in the plains as a grazing country; but the plains as a farming country will not sustain it long.
>
> So if we were asked to designate the three most characteristic animals of the plains today we could not name the same animals listed fifty years ago. During that time, the hand of man has fallen heavily on the dominant animals, and we will have to step down several grades to choose from more insignificant animals. We may retain in our list the coyote, the most contemptible of the old time triad, but in place of the lordly buffalo, we must substitute a "barking squirrel," as the prairie dog was termed in the Lewis & Clark expedition; instead of the antelope, we must accept the almost equally fleet, but much smaller jackrabbit. We still retain, however, the division of the three into one predatory and two fugitive animals. . . .
>
> The Mexicans call the jackrabbit "Liebre," as distinguished from "conejo," a cottontail rabbit. Both

words are derived from the Latin, in which "lepus" stands for hare and "cuniculus" for rabbit. The word "coney," used by the English to designate a rabbit, comes from the same source. The distinction between the two animals is called to the attention of every Englishman, as both are common in his country.

The jackrabbit is "facile princeps" (the first), in speed and continuous movement. It possesses that ability almost to the extent of the horse. No bounds are set on its appropriation of new territory. It needs water much more than a cottontail rabbit, but access to water or lack of it does not seem to be a consideration when it invades a new province. It has penetrated the dryest part of our area, and left unmolested those portions where water can be found in abundance.

The natural inference is that arid and semi-arid countries, where it is found in greatest abundance, are the countries best suited to its increase, and therefore, it is not adaptable to a humid climate. Since the animal requires water, humidity alone can hardly be directly responsible for these circumstances. It is rarely found living more than five or six miles from surface water and is found in great abundance in the vicinity of water. Perhaps there are secondary causes which are responsible for its living in such arid climates. These areas may contain the vegetation it needs for sustenance, or this type of environment may not be conducive to the growth and activity of the jackrabbit's enemies. There may be several reasons of which we are not aware.

The jackrabbit is apparently one of our oldest inhabitants. We find it present in the very earliest historical accounts of the Trans-Pecos country. Cabeza de Vaca is believed to have passed through the southern part of Pecos County in 1534, only 14 years after Cortez had conquered Mexico. While in this area, de Vaca reported: "Hares were very abundant. The Indians were armed with clubs, which they throw with great precision and killed more hares than the party could consume. When one was started they would surround and attack it with their clubs, driving it from one to another until it was overcome and captured."

This account tallies well with the stories I have been told by the older Mexicans in our area. I had found a round stone about the size of a hen's egg in a great many graves in this country believed to be of Mescalero Indian origin. It was not a stone found any place in Pecos County. It was one of the pitted and flecked stones found in the volcanic region around Fort Davis and Alpine, apparently tufaceous, and often found in the water courses of that vicinity — more or less rounded by the action of water for thousands of years. I was well enough acquainted with the mortuary customs of these Indians to know that it must have had some use in the daily life of these people.

When I inquired about the use of this stone, elderly Mexicans told me that it was used as a club in the following manner: It was covered and sewed in with rawhides and attached by a short thong of the same rawhide to a stick of about 12 inches in length. The stick was used as a handle. It was thrown with great accuracy at hares, quails and rabbits, and was a favorite weapon for use in hunting small game. I have heard further that this kind of weapon was used by the Sioux Indians in going over Custer's last battlefield to crush in the skulls of any of the unfortunate soldiers who showed signs of life. It was used in this last instance as an economy, rather than the more rare powder and shot, and in de Vaca's time it was used probably in the same spirit of economy, rather than risk the loss and destruction of the stone arrow heads in shooting with the bow. For it was probably the "club" mentioned in de Vaca's account, and if so, then it is apparent that hares were not only abundant, but also were tamer than in these days.

With the passing of the Mescaleros, the animal ceased to be a game animal. It is not esteemed as a food by either Mexican or American, and no great hunts have been organized after the ancient Indian fashion to drive it by means of a narrowing circle of hunters into some trap, as has been a custom with

Americans in Colorado and California. Here, it is not a menace to any industry, as it is in those countries, and it has not yet been found necessary to resort to such methods to check the increase of the animal.

Yet it has its destructive habits. It consumes the grass in pastures, and if there are enough jackrabbits, this represents considerable monetary loss. Our farmers can verify its destructiveness to growing crops such as corn, cotton, wheat, alfalfa, etc., in the early stages of growth. Indeed, between the ravages of jackrabbits on the young plant, and those of the crow and blackbird on the ripening grain, farmers raising milo maize, Kaffir corn and other sorghum crops in this county must fight incessantly to save their produce.

As far as I can judge from personal observation for the past 25 years, the numerical status of the jackrabbit has remained fairly constant in Pecos County. The population fluctuates some during wet or dry seasons. A dry season causes a decrease in the following year, while a wet season generally results in an increase. The variation in numbers is not great. However, at times, special causes are introduced which do reduce the numbers of the animal. The most notable of these within my recollection was the epidemic of 1890 and 1891.

This caused great mortality in the northern part of the county, to which I was a witness. Whether it extended to other parts of the county, and to other counties, I do not know, as I didn't travel about during that period. But along the Pecos River from Horsehead Crossing to Pecos City, the hares died by the thousands. A greater abundance of carcasses were found in the vicinity of the water courses than in any other areas, which probably indicated the effects of fever. Some of the animals appeared to have suffered from malnutrition for some time, while others were fat when they died. The plague lasted during four or five months of the spring and early summer, and when it ceased, it was apparently because there were no more hares in that section of the country.

We never knew the cause of this great desolation. We presumed that it was a contagious disease of some kind, but further than this had nothing on which to speculate. The origin of the disease remained a mystery to us — as did the sudden cessation of the plague. Indeed, it may have been purely local. In those days our communications system left something to be desired, and the scattered inhabitants of the country had not yet professed any great interest in the condition of minor animals. The plague came and went, without much more significant remark than that of old Bonifacio Cardenas, who "wished that I had some dogs so I could have something to feed on all those dead hares."

Had Bonifacio possessed some dogs to eat those dead hares, more than likely his dogs would have keeled over as dead as the hares.

Four years after Judge Williams wrote this article the cause of the disease was discovered. Originally called "deer fly fever," it was first observed by Ancil Martin, an Arizona physician, who traced the infection to skinning and dressing wild rabbits. By 1910 the disease was so serious in southern California that the United States Public Health Service sent two surgeons to investigate. The infection was found to be prevalent in ground squirrels inhabiting the bulrushes (called tules by the early Spanish settlers). The technical name for the disease, tularemia, comes from that plant.

The most important contribution to research on that disease was made by the medical director of the United States Public Health Service, Edward Francis, who contracted tularemia during his studies. The specific cause of the disease is the bacterium tularense, which is transmitted to man by the bites of flies and ticks. The symptoms are frightful headache, prolonged fever, and swollen lymph glands which may suppurate and require incision.

During our operations west of Fort Stockton, we noticed a large number of jackrabbits in 1946 with lumps on their bodies. The animals looked rather sick and crippled and were evidently suffering from tularemia. The following quote is from the *Scientific Monthly*, November, 1928.

> Don't touch a wild rabbit that seems dull, dopey, glassy-eyed, slow moving or with rough, ragged fur. Don't fail to shoot such rabbits or those that won't run from you on sight. When killed, either burn or bury them, lest dogs or cats contract the disease by eating the carcass. Don't use a rabbit or handle one caught or killed and brought home by the children or family dog. They were probably too sick to run from them. Don't handle or touch a wild rabbit, unless with rubber gloves.

So one now knows why the jackrabbit should never be used for human consumption. Previously, the mere fact that the animal frequently carried unexplained lumps on its body was sufficient reason for man to abhor it, or shudder at the idea of eating its flesh.

Travis Roberts, of Marathon, told me that one of his uncles became infected with tularemia by skinning and dressing a rabbit in Brewster County. It must have been a cottontail rabbit, as few people ever touched the meat of a jackrabbit. He recovered after a prolonged, serious illness.

Ox warble is another cause of lumps on rabbits. T. W. Hillin, a former county agent of Pecos County, told me that the heel fly causes lumps under the skin of rabbits and other animals. It is called heel fly because it deposits eggs about the size and color of a grain of sugar on the hair of the heels of animals. When transferred to the animal's stomach by mouth, the ox warble larva develops into a worm and bores its way upward until it reaches a place under the skin. There it forms a lump, inside of which the worm will be found. This lump on rabbits can sometimes be mistaken for the disease tularemia.

Judge Williams continues writing on the jackrabbit:

> The jackrabbit grazes and relies on grass as its

main food. We have several varieties of grass in this county, but so far as I have observed, it shows no marked preference for any one brand, but eats them all impartially. When a drouth hits and grass loses its succulence, the rabbit turns to shrubs and herbs for its sustenance. During these periods it loses flesh and strength and becomes an easy victim of the coyote and lynx. During a protracted drouth it often perishes of starvation. I am inclined to believe that the periodical return of long spring or summer drouths in this section of the country do more to control the rabbit population than all other natural causes acting together.

Possibly due to the limited range of its commissariat it is very willing to experiment on new types of vegetation. The farmer will find it nibbling on any and every kind of new crop which he may choose to plant, and if the new plant proves appetizing, he may find that he has the jackrabbit to fight if he hopes to have any harvest. It is especially partial to young alfalfa, and will not only eat the top growth down to the ground, but will scratch down in the ground after the root. It also eats other root crops, such as beets, turnips, etc. It does most of its foraging at night, and during the day it lies in its forms [the lair or hiding place of a hare].

Jackrabbits are easy to kill at night while they are eating. Farmers can carry lanterns into their alfalfa, cotton or other fields and approach almost within striking distance of the jacks. If a second party carries a gun along a number of the animals can be destroyed. I have found that they can also be poisoned, as I was once quite successful in destroying a large number of them with strychnine. In the light of the full moon, these furry scamps were making a most determined attack on my cabbage patch. I placed the poison on watermelon rinds and set them along the outer edge of the cabbage patch. They may eat through the outside rind of a watermelon, but I have never found the evidence. Nevertheless, the juicy meat of the melon is most tempting to them when it is open to their assault. They seem to have an investigative attitude toward their food and never fail to taste and test any new growth of vegetation within their territory.

My friend, D. C. McAteer, a cotton farmer in Pecos County, complains bitterly of difficulty with the little varmints on his stand of cotton. When the tender plant is small, the jack nips off its top. When the plant grows large it bores through the stem with its sharp teeth and eats only the stem. It doesn't touch the remainder of the plant which it has destroyed.

I never grew enough cotton to experience that problem, but the furry little rogues attacked my alfalfa and hegari fields. During one of their perennial population explosions, I placed pieces of poisoned apples around the perimeter of my large tract of alfalfa. I was finally forced to place an eighteen-inch rabbit fence around the field and call up a rabbit drive to catch and kill the jackrabbits caught in such enclosures. These drives have been held at various times by Pecos County ranchers to eliminate what seemed to be an excess population of rabbits.

Judge Williams' article continues:

> I think the animal must be guided to some extent by its sense of smell in the investigation of new food. The nostrils seem to be very sensitive and are in constant agitation while it is engaged in browsing, which has led me to believe that it chooses its food largely by the aid of smell. Further, it must depend upon the use of that sense to a very large extent in night feeding. In the case of the poisoned watermelon rind, it must have been attracted to the rind because of the odor. Certainly the taste could not have been the sense relied on by the animal, as it is well known that strychnine adds a most bitter, unpleasant taste to any article of food permeated with it.
>
> During the day, the animal hides in its form around a bush or a shrub, and in some places under a clump of grass. This form generally faces toward

the north, less often toward the east and west, and more rarely toward the south. It seems to spend no more time scratching out or shaping its resting place than a hen does in making her nest. In fact, it has much the appearance of a nest, but it is longer and not as rounded in shape as a hen's nest. A cover of grass or twigs will be found growing just as nature dictated, without any artificial arrangement or disposition on the part of our hare. It seems to have done nothing more than to have selected a spot covered by grass or shrubbery and to have scratched there a small resting place which fits the form of its body.

Sometimes this covering of grass or shrub seems to me so slight as to cause me to wonder how it could be considered a protection. A wisp of grass, a fragile branch of an annual herb; these would seem to offer no protection against the talons of a hawk in its powerful downward sweep, yet the jackrabbit hides there in perfect confidence, as if embowered in the thorny mazes of a tecumblate shrub [probably the javelina bush, or little buckthorn — microrhamnus ericoides], or harbored under the stubborn arm of a mesquite bush.

Probably the presence of the hare in its flimsy form is very easily detected by the keen eye of the hawk as it sails effortlessly over the countryside reconnoitering for food. Certainly I have seen hawks sailing over the covert in such a manner as to indicate that the hare was spotted, but there was that protective cover, and the bird was apparently searching for a position where that cover would not intervene between it and the quarry. To the bird, a wisp of grass or the branch of a dead herb might appear as dangerous an obstacle as the thorny bower of tecumblates, or the rigid arm of the cat-claw. The rabbit form is no more improbable than many another device of protective imitation accepted by naturalists as an adaptation of defense by inferior animals or birds.

For example, we are told that the blotched white wings of a certain butterfly afford protection to the insect from the attack of birds. Supposedly, this causes it to resemble bird lime. The coloring is the result of natural selection acting to bring about what is called a mimicry protection. The protection that fragile grass or weeds gives to a hare can just as certainly and properly be called a mimicry protection. In both cases the protection is due to an appearance which is misleading. The substance of the protection is safety to the intended prey, yet the frail covering is only a semblance of safety; it is a mere shadow between the rapacious hawk and the timid rabbit — but that shadow acts as effectively as a material body. The straws of grass over the little rabbit bar the hawk from making its aerial plunge as finally as if they were the solid wood of mesquite limbs. This is solely because the appearance of the grass mimics that of a branch of the mesquite bush.

Our jackrabbit can lay claim to leading a strenuous life after the most approved Rooseveltian [Teddy] style. He is in constant danger. In this country, it would seem that at some bygone day Mother Nature opened a Pandora's box of evils for our frisky friend with the burro ears. First an animal darts at old Jack; then a bird swoops after him; and along comes a reptile, and if none of these ends his career, a drouth hits and depletes his food supply. He then finds life's tenuous strings snapping under the pressure of starvation. The coyote runs the poor little rabbit a long and weary chase; the lynx lies in wait for it at the crossroads; and the evil swish of a hawk's wings fills it with panic by day, while the ominous clack of the owl's bill haunts it by night. It has no city of peace or refuge. No caves offer hospitable comfort; no holes in the ground furnish rest and safety. On the open plains it must depend almost solely upon those tireless leg sinews, and that light, lean body in its struggle for survival. Made in the mould of the race horse, its motto might be "Speed, speed, always speed!"

If a jackrabbit burrows a hole, or uses a hole already burrowed, I have never seen the evidence. In fact, the books state that one of the distinctive differences between a hare and a rabbit is that the latter burrows, while the former does not. Yet I am led to suspect that at times the jackrabbit surely must have recourse to an underground burrow. During some five and twenty years of residence in this country, with much of my life spent in the open I have never found the small young of the animal. I have always first noticed the young hares when they were about two-thirds grown and fairly able to take care of themselves. Now why is it that the small animals are not to be seen if they do not take refuge in holes?

I gather that when the animal is quite young it probably depends entirely on the mother's milk and does not stir away from whatever hiding place she has selected. Later, when it begins to graze upon herbs and browse upon shrubs, mama probably takes it out by night to teach it its first lessons. We see it for the first time in the light of day, taking its place with its brothers when she has abandoned it as a well educated youngster able to fend for itself. Certainly its life during this period of nurture is well concealed from the eyes of man and the beasts and birds of prey, otherwise hares would soon be extinct. However, this period may not be spent underground. The mother may make her nest in clumps of grass. Little Jack may spend his early life in a small grass covered house so cunningly made that passersby may see nothing but some dead grass. I do not know how the rabbit conceals its young.

I have mentioned above that the reptile is one of the hare's numerous enemies. The motive of the reptile, of course, is hunger, and hunger only, so it is easily understood that the young of the jackrabbit would be the special object of the reptile's hunt. Being helpless and left to themselves, they would fall easy victims. In addition, they would be a nice size for ingestion for snakes in this region. There is no snake in this country which can swallow a full grown jackrabbit, yet I have heard of many incidents of snakes making prey of these full grown animals without being able to use them for food. I shall relate one of these incidents, as tending to illustrate a curious power of some snakes, or perhaps I better say a curious weakness of the hare in the presence of the rattlesnake. Mr. and Mrs. Drew Taylor were on the Pecos

River near Grandfalls in 1890. They drove down the river one day in a buggy and on their drive witnessed the following incident which they related to me on their return: Some miles down river they saw a rattlesnake off to the side of the road. The snake was so intent on something in front of it that it paid not the slightest attention to the horses and buggy only a few feet away. This particular snake is a sluggish creature, not capable of very rapid movement except when it strikes. Yet, this snake was evidently moving as rapidly as possible, with its head held low and close to the ground in a direction parallel to the road.

Looking forward some 20 feet in the line of the snake's motion they saw a full grown jackrabbit huddled in its form, under a clump of salt grass. The terrified animal was trembling all over; its ears were drooping and it was plainly in a state of great excitement. Yet it remained immobile, apparently unable to move, until the snake came within reach and delivered its stroke. Then the jackrabbit leaped into the air with an almost human scream and fell on its side. The snake seized it and coiled around it. The spectators then killed the snake without waiting to observe further proceedings. This was apparently comparable to those stories of birds which fall prey to the snake under some similar loss of nerve control. I have heard other stories of a similar nature, but I have not witnessed anything of the kind in my own experience.

It is not unusual to find a large rattlesnake or bull snake that has swallowed a small cottontail or jackrabbit. Jack Silliman, engineer, surveyor and contractor in Fort Stockton, relates a story concerning this phenomenon. While surveying, he found a large rattlesnake. His rodman placed the butt of the rod on the snake's head to hold it until Jack could attempt to pop its head off — a feat he had heard about. Jack grabbed the snake's tail, whirled the reptile rapidly like a whip and gave a stout backward jerk, expecting to see its head fly off. Something did plop on the ground, but Jack's attention was riveted on the snake, which he was still holding — its head was intact, although the rattler seemed to be rather ill. Again he popped the snake like a whip, and a small rabbit fell out of the snake's mouth. This time when he looked down at the snake it was sick, but had a vengeful gleam in its eye as if it were ready for action. He threw it down and killed it, but during the whip-popping show the snake had disgorged two small rabbits.

The cottontail rabbit is found throughout the Americas, from Alaska to Patagonia. He is a short, chunky little fellow, much smaller and less bony and angular than his cousin Jack. The cottontail burrows into the ground to build its nest when its young are born. It is reported that the small, spirited mothers will attempt to protect their babies from snakes or varmints by kicking the intruders. Cottontails prefer the brush country where their quick movements and change of direction allow them to avoid their pursuers.

The inimitable Bugs Bunny would want this chapter closed with humor, so I give you the following anecdote:

The family of the late Judge Jackson included his wife, four boys and a girl. They kept greyhounds for the sport of running jackrabbits. This family amused one another with liberal doses of dry wit.

One day Mrs. Jackson observed her boys preparing to take the dogs and chase rabbits. She cautioned, "Barney, look out for snakes."

Barney quipped, "All right, Mama, how many do you want?"

The Peccary
(Tayassuidae)

According to scientists there are three suborders of living artiodactyls: Suiformes, Tylopoda and Ruminantia. The suborder of Suiformes includes pigs, peccaries and hippos, which have a large variety of forms. The shape of teeth varies greatly from species to species. In some of these animals the stomach is simple, while in others it is divided into compartments. The peccary or javelina has small eyes on a cone-shaped head with nostrils ending on a flat-surfaced nose. It is almost the size and shape of a pig. The ears stand up or fold over slightly and the tail is short. The thick skin is covered with bristles, and the short, strong limbs end in four toes, only two of which are functional.

195

The collared peccary (Tayassu tajacu) is similar to the European wild boar and lives from Texas, New Mexico and Arizona south to Patagonia. In West Texas, it is known by its Mexican name "javelina." Javelinas live in bands of twenty-five or more and eat cactus, fruits, berries, tubers, rhizomes and even grub the roots of the lechuguilla. Their well-developed canines grow down rather than up, as in other wild suids.

If left alone, they avoid people, but if one is wounded, the hunter may find himself attacked by the entire herd. Armed with two large, sharp tusks which are quite dangerous, the swift, agile javelina is more than a match for a coyote, bobcat or dog. Like other West Texas animals, they are equipped with a musk gland that emits a repugnant scent which discourages the hunter from seeking its meat. The musk gland, similar in appearance to an enlarged navel, is located on the back, several inches in front of the hip bones. Once this gland is removed from the carcass, the meat is reported to be savory.

The animal has no scruples about trampling down the farmer's grain and other crops and helping itself to food. I understand javelinas are now bred in some places for their meat and their hides. The hides are used for making gloves and shoes.

Local ranchers report that when raised in captivity, the animals make excellent watchdogs. On the other side of the ledger, some ranchmen are certain that javelinas kill and eat goats and sheep.

Claude Owens, who ranches about fifty miles east of Fort Stockton, related a bit of information to me about javelinas. Many years ago, his father's ranch hand heard a loud outcry which sounded as if it came from the top of a mesa above the ranch headquarters. Very shortly he heard another agonizing cry. He saddled his horse and rode toward the sound. Upon arrival he found two freshly killed goats and saw a number of others being herded along the fence by some javelinas.

Loren Hillger and his wife run the Girl Scout Hat-A-Ranch about forty-five miles southeast of Fort Stockton. Some of the Girl Scouts brought a small kid goat to the camp and left it there when they returned home. One day, Loren and his wife were discussing the probability that javelinas kill livestock. During the discussion, Loren glanced out the window and saw the kid goat jumping and dodging about in the low brush. Out of curiosity he went out to check on the goat. When he drew near he saw javelinas charging the goat one at a time. The active kid was easily dodging its assailants; nevertheless, it eagerly ran to its master for safety.

Evidently the javelina is quite wary of man, for I have heard of only two instances when one attacked or charged a man. (We shall overlook the Big Foot Wallace story that I shall quote later.) A friend of mine, Pockets Moore, reported that while he was on top of the Seven Mile Mesa, east of Fort Stockton, he found a baby javelina. Out of curiosity he picked it up.

The little pig squealed in terror, and all the adult javelinas immediately gave chase. Pockets dropped the baby pig, but the angry adults continued their pursuit. Feeling razor-sharp teeth closing in on him, Pockets raced for the edge of the caprock and leaped off without a backward glance.

Fortunately he landed about twenty feet below — unfortunately he also landed in a thick growth of prickly pear. This cushioned his fall, but for the next two weeks Pockets was busy pulling prickly pear thorns out of his body.

My grandson, Clayton Pollard, then only twelve years old, told me the following story about his almost fatal incident with a javelina on the old Dick Arnold ranch south of Fort Stockton:

> I was at my Uncle Claytie's deer camp some forty-five miles south of Fort Stockton. It was December 1972. I had shot my deer that morning and in the afternoon I had nothing to do but hunt anything I

could find. We, my brother, Scott, Teddy LaCaff and I, were going down a dirt road and decided that the three of us would walk to a hill about one hundred yards away. We couldn't drive up because there was a fence between us and the hill.

We hadn't walked very far when Scott spotted some javelinas. The animals were so far off on the top of the hill I don't know how he saw them. We then planned for me to run to the other side of the hill and Scott and Teddy to stay on this side. In this way we might get a shot at them. I started off to the right side of the hill at a good distance so I wouldn't frighten them away. About fifteen minutes later I got to the hill and saw the javelinas slowly moving up the hill and about to cross over to the other side. I didn't have time to go around so I slowly started up the hill.

I got about a hundred yards from them and they were almost out of sight. I figured I couldn't get any closer without scaring them and I could see seven. There was a ridge on top of the hill that was too steep for them to get over so I didn't think they could get through or over and would have to stay on my side of the hill.

I was carrying a 30-30 Winchester rifle that would not eject the shell after it had been fired and I had to use my knife to pry the shell out. I hid behind a big rock, took careful aim and fired my first shot. The javelina I shot at didn't go down but limped off and the other javelinas started running. The shell was stuck in my gun so I got out my knife and pried it out. I knew the javelinas were getting away so I didn't take time to put the knife up. I just set it down by the big rock and started running after the javelinas as they were charging through a break in the ridge. I took a shot at the hindmost animal. It fell down and then got up and got into high speed again. I followed them through the break in the ridge.

On the other side of the ridge it was more abrupt in its decline and much brushier and I couldn't see a javelina. I thought I had lost them so I started walking slowly across the top of the hill. I walked up about four feet from a big grey bush and stopped. I stood there for only a moment when I heard a rustle in the brush beside me. In that instant I turned my head just in time to see a javelina lunging out of the brush at my legs. I could almost feel those razor-sharp tusks slashing at me. I let out a yell of fear and jumped. I looked back over my shoulder and saw the animal pass and barely brush the back of my legs.

When I came down from my jump and turned, I saw the javelina stumble and roll about ten feet away. I pointed my gun at him and pulled the trigger. It clicked. I tried to eject the shell but it was stuck. I didn't have my knife. That fraction of a second seemed like forever until I dug the shell out with my thumb nail and put in another one. With careful aim I shot him just as he was getting up to charge me.

Upon examining his body, I found that it was the one I had previously wounded because his left side had been injured by that shot. That injury likely prevented him from turning to the left when I jumped, or he would have cut me to pieces.

Still scared, I walked carefully along the top of the ridge, looking for the other javelinas. I came to a small cave. Inside it was the other wounded javelina. I shot him.

It was a big story when I got back to camp.

Big Foot Wallace was expert at spinning a tale, even if he had to add some incidents to it — but when John C. Duval got hold of it and polished it up a bit it became a classic. The following story is their tale about a poor greenhorn author who intended to write a book and was doing his research on a trip with Wallace. The setting of the tale is in country similar to that around the Pecos or Devil's Rivers. It is as greatly exaggerated as the tale of the untimely death of Mark Twain, but here we go:

> Our author was a great geologist, I think he called it, as well as a bookmaker. He would frequently talk to me about the "stratas" and the "primary" and

"tertiary" formations, though I told him I did not know anything of such matters; and whenever we stopped to camp, he would frequently "boge" about for hours among the caverns and gulches, hunting what he called "specimens," and come back with his pockets filled with rocks, which he would sort out and label and then store them away carefully in his saddlebags. On one occasion I heard one of my men say to another, "Bill, what in the thunder do you suppose the 'author' has got in his saddle-wallets, that makes them so heavy?"

"Don't know," said Bill, "unless they are nuggets."

"Nuggets?" said the other, "they are rocks just like these you see laying all around here. I know it is so, for I looked into them this morning!"

"Why," answered Bill, "what do you reckon the fool is packing them about for?"

"No idea," said the other, "unless he has no faith in that 'bird-gun' and 'pepper-box' [derringer] he totes, and intends to fight with them when we catch up with these Injuns. The truth is, Bill," he continued, "the fellow is crazy as a bed-bug, sure, and if he only had any weapons about that could hurt a body, I should keep my eye skinned on him, certain."

In fact, by this time the belief was prevalent among the men that our author was really "unsettled" in his mind, which supposition preceeded, in the end, to be of service to him, for of course they could not hold a crazy man responsible for anything he did.

As soon after our halt as he had unsaddled and staked his horse, he went out, as usual, hunting "specimens" in the ravines and gullies among the hills. I was just settling myself upon my blanket, to take a comfortable snooze, when we heard him "halloo" repeatedly about half a mile from camp.

"There," said one of the men, "there is that crazy chap got into a scrape with another buck, I suppose, and somebody will have to go and help him out of it."

"Yes," said another, "and the first thing he knows he will have his hair lifted 'boging' about alone, with nothing but that 'pop-gun' of his to fight with. He had better trust to his 'umbrella.'"

I was satisfied, however, it could not be a buck that was after him this time, for I had noticed, when he left camp, that he did not take his "pop-gun" along with him, and as he continued to "sing out" louder and louder, I at length picked up my rifle, and started off to see what sort of a scrape he had got into. At the bottom of a deep ravine, I found him sitting on the top of a chaparral bush, with his memorandum book in his hand, and about a dozen Mexican hogs around him. He was barely out of their reach, and every now and then, one of them would make a pass at his legs, whenever he stretched them down to relieve them a little from the constrained position in which he was compelled to keep them.

As soon as I appreciated the situation of affairs, I scrambled up into a mesquite tree, about thirty paces from where our author was roosting, for I knew very well these "havilinas," when excited and roused, were the most dangerous of all our wild animals. When in considerable numbers, they frequently attack a man with great ferocity, and are almost certain to cut him to pieces with their terrible tusks, unless he can effect a timely retreat, for they are much more active and swift on foot than the common wild hog.

When I found myself safe from their attack, I called out to our author to know what he was doing on the top of that bush.

"Hallo! Captain!" He called out, "Is that you?" (For the hogs had kept him so busy he had not noticed me till then.) "I am as glad to see you as I was when the buck was after me. I hope, though you will not be quite so deliberate as you were on that occasion."

"Yes," I answered, "but what are you doing on the top of that bush?"

"Doing!" said he. "Can't you see that I am trying to keep my legs out of reach of these outrageous wild pigs, and it is as much as I can do at that. There! Did you see that scoundrel make a pass at me?"

"Why don't you drive them away?" I asked.

"Drive them away!" cried the author. "I have thrown all my specimens at them, and everything else I had about me except my memorandum book, and it only makes them worse. They are not afraid of anything."

Said I, "Mr. Author," fixing myself comfortably on a limb, "this reminds me of a scrape I once got into with these 'havilinas' that would do for a chapter in the *Wayworn Wanderer*; and as we are comfortably fixed out here, all by ourselves, I could not have a better chance of telling it to you."

"Comfortable!" he exclaimed. "You have strange ideas of it, if you think a man can be comfortable sitting on top of your abominable Texas chaparral, with his knees drawn up to his chin, a thorn in each leg as long as my finger, and a dozen wild hogs making lunges at them whenever he stretches them down for a moment's ease. For heaven's sake, shoot them," he implored, "and let me out of this nest of thorns."

"I can't," I replied, "I have only the bullet that is in the gun, and if I shoot one of them, it will make the rest ten times worse."

"You don't tell me so, Captain," he answered, "then what in the world shall we do?"

"Why," said I, "the only thing we can do now is to be patient, and wait until the moon rises tonight, and I think then the 'havilinas' will leave us."

"Oh! Don't talk to me about the moon's rising. It won't be up till twelve o'clock, at least, and I can't stand this fifteen minutes longer, no how. Cracky! That fellow gave me a grazer! He has taken off the heel of my boot on his tusks!"

"You see, Mr. Author," I continued, pretending not to hear what he said, "it was about six years ago, that Bill Hankins and I were out 'bear hunting' on the headwaters of the Leon, when — "

"Plague take that fellow, he brought blood that time, certain!" said our author. "Their teeth are as sharp as razors. They are gnawing my bush down. They will have it down in less than ten minutes," said the author, in a pitiable tone.

"As I was saying," I continued, "it was about six years ago that Bill Hankins and I were out bear hunting on the headwaters of the Leon, when we fell in with a large drove of 'havilinas.' "

"Shoo! You devils!" said our author, flinging his last missile, his memorandum book, at the hogs, as they made a general rush on his bush.

"Mr. Author," I said, in an offended tone, "you are not paying the slightest attention to what I am telling you. You might learn something even from the Indians in this respect, for, according to Mr. Cooper, they never interrupt a man when he is talking.

"As I was saying," I continued, "it was about six years ago that Bill Hankins and I were out bear hunting on the headwaters of the Leon — "

"Oh! Bother Mr. Cooper and Bill Hankins and the headwaters of the Leon," said our author, losing his temper at my persistence in relating the anecdote. "Cooper's a fool. Oh, My! There's a thorn clean through my back, into the hollow!"

"But, my friend," said I, changing my tactics, "you ought to bear your troubles with patience, for you should remember what a thrilling chapter you will be able to make out of this adventure for the *Wayworn Wanderer.*"

"Oh, yes," said he, "but who would there be to write it, when I am chawed up by those infuriated pigs like a handful of acorns? Oh, dear! They'll have me directly. I can feel the bush giving away now. Captain," said he, "you will find the manuscript of the *Wayworn Wanderer* in my saddlebags. Take it, and publish it for the benefit of the world, and tell them of the melancholy fate of the poor author. But tell them, for mercy's sake, that I was devoured by a lion, or a panther, or a catamount, or some other decent sort of a beast, and not by a gang of squealing pigs. It won't sound romantic, you know."

"I'll do it, Mr. Author," said I, "but I hope you will live long enough yet to tell them all about it yourself. You have a first-rate chance now to study the habits and appearance of these 'havilinas,' and can write a chapter on them that will be very interesting, and true to nature. How will you describe them?" I asked.

"They look to me," he answered, "like a couple of

butcher knives about as long as my arm, stuck into a handle covered with hair and bristles!"

"And can you tell me," I said, "what particular tribe of animals they belong to?"

"Captain," he answered, "I don't feel inclined to discuss the subject just now, particularly as the subject is so eager to discuss me, and besides, to tell you the truth, I think you have selected a most unsuitable time for propounding your questions in natural history. Oh, my! There goes the leg of my pants, and a strip of the hide with it!"

"Mr. Author," I said pretending not to hear his remarks, "I recollect once reading a chapter in one of Mr. Cooper's novels, in which he gives a very interesting account of the immense droves of wild pigeons that were migrating from one part of the country to another, and — "

"Oh, bother Cooper, I say!" said our author, becoming perfectly frantic, as a thorn touched him up in the rear, and a pig made a dash at his legs in front. "Cooper is an unmitigated humbug, and I begin to think you are not much better. Oh, I can stand this no longer," said he, "and I'll make a finish of it at once," and I verily believe he would have jumped down right among the hogs in another moment, but just then I saw several of my men coming toward us from camp, and said to him:

"Hold on a minute, Mr. Author, there come some men to help us, and we'll soon rout the beasts now." Seeing that we were both treed by some sort of "varmints," the men hurried up, shot several of the hogs, and the balance, finding we mustered too strong for them, quickly retreated into the chaparral.

Cimarrons or Big Horn Sheep
(Bovidae, bovinae, antilopinae)

The Bovinae is a member of the Bovidae or ox family of ruminants. Characteristically, it has a pair of hollow, unbranched horns, and the species includes cattle, sheep, goats, and antelopes. A subfamily, Antilopinae, includes animals with ringed horns, snouts, hair up to the rims of the nostrils and short tails. There are fourteen genera in this family of goats or sheep. They are generally found in the wild and are exceptionally sure-footed animals.

Reportedly there were mountain or big horn sheep in

the Big Bend of Texas prior to the time game hunters or predators exterminated them.

Let Judge Williams give his information of 1908:

> I have headed this chapter, "Cimarron," which is the Mexican appellation for the animal that we know as the Big Horn or Rocky Mountain Sheep. . . .
>
> Many years ago, while traveling on the Cimarron River in New Mexico, I inquired as to the meaning of the river's name. I was told that the word was coined in the New World by the Mexicans who had named the river after the Big Horn Sheep because they were abundant on the headwaters of the river. Subsequently, I heard the name applied to the Big Horn Sheep in New Mexico and in Trans-Pecos Texas, and I never heard them use any other Mexican name. Naturally I concluded that this distinctive name was applicable only to the Big Horn, and that they had sole and exclusive right to the title.
>
> I was shocked out of this belief after reading George Byam's account of his life in Central America. Byam stated that 80 years ago, the wild cattle in that country were termed "Cimarrones." Still later, I discovered that the name applied to wild horses in South America. When the word was introduced into the English language it was disguised, hammered into shape and the spelling was altered.
>
> By applying what we have heretofore found on the Spanish meaning of the word, I think we can reasonably surmise that the name was originally "Borregos Cimarrone," or "Wild Sheep." We can probably also conclude that in time the adjective not only fulfilled its own purpose, but qualified as a noun and turned the old, longer name out into the cold.
>
> To my knowledge, the first mention of the Big Horn Sheep is in Castaneda's account of Coronado's expedition to New Mexico and Kansas in 1540. This military expedition was made about 20 years after Cortez conquered Mexico. Castaneda took cannon and vast stores of supplies to conquer the Buffalo King-

dom. In those plains, this was somewhat like a mirage — always dancing ahead of them at an uncertain distance and in uncertain shapes. At times the men were sorely at a loss to retrace their steps, and Castaneda says: ". . . who could believe that 1,000 horses, and 500 of our cows, and more than 5,000 rams and ewes and more than 1,500 friendly Indians and servants in traveling over these plains, would leave no more trace where they had passed than if nothing had been there — so that it was necessary to make piles of bones and cow chips now and then so that the rear guard could follow the army!"

What was more natural than for Castaneda's comrades to have called these Big Horns "Borregos Cimarrones — Sheep Wild"? They were in such contrast with the tame sheep they had brought with them. The name "Cimarron" probably originated then and there when the Spaniards applied this term to the animal.

So much for the name; now let us turn to the animal. At various times during the past 25 years I have heard that the horns of Cimarrons had been found along the Rio Grande, between the mouth of San Francisco Creek and the Pecos River. However, I cannot recall anyone who claims to have seen them in that country. It is not improbable to believe that they were there 20 years ago, and possibly, a few may yet be in that region. The area is very rugged and rocky with the type of terrain that is not conducive to settlement. Unless exterminated by persistent hunters, small numbers of the sheep could survive for quite a long time. The hunter who would trek up and down the cragged border of the Rio Grande would have to possess great patience, intestinal fortitude, and a strong constitution. He would have need of all of those qualities in abundance. The unlimited climbing involved in hunting in this region would discourage most men.

Reportedly the Big Horn was found in the Grand Canyon of the Rio Grande in 1901. According to reliable sources, a herd of 40 or 50 animals were in the canyon, although I did not see them. The canyon is about seven miles long from the river's entrance below Lajitas to its exit at the mouth of the Terlinqua Creek. It is only 12 miles from the quicksilver mines which have been in operation more than ten years. At times these mines have supported a population of 600 or 700 people. The Mexican town of San Carlos lies 20 miles away in Chihuahua. The Grand Canyon once bore the name Canyon de Agulo after a Mexican man named Agulo. Local folklore credits Agulo with the feat of preserving his stock year after year from Comanche raids. During the time of the Mexican moon, as the Comanches termed their raiding month, he placed his stock in the canyon. It is such an inaccessible area that the Big Horns have managed to exist in spite of the proximity of civilized settlements. In this country, for many years, $25 has been the standing offer for a good head from a male Big Horn, and one can understand that the Grand Canyon is not good hunting ground, otherwise the market would have been flooded.

In about 1886, Francis Rooney was living at Leoncita Springs. According to Rooney, a herd of about 15 Big Horns had recently been spotted in the Glass Mountains. They were on the border between Pecos County and present Brewster County. If anyone has seen them lately, I have not heard about it. Many people doubt that there were ever any Big Horn in these mountains due to the absence of water in that vicinity. I cannot personally vouch for the validity of the statement that there is no living water in the mountains, but I have never found any, nor heard of anyone who has. It is universally conceded that the mountains contain no living water. Even admitting that proposition, it does not justify the doubt concerning the Big Horn. There are many wild animals in Pecos County which evidently do not depend on living water.

About fifteen or twenty years ago the Park Service

placed a number of big horn sheep in the Big Bend Park in Texas. I understand as long as they were fenced in and protected from predators the herd multiplied. However, the herd was turned loose without protection, and recently I have been told that their number has decreased.

The Prairie Dog
(Cyonomys ludovicianus)

This short-legged, stout little animal is actually a burrowing squirrel, rather than a dog, with a three-inch black tail. It inhabits the plains and plateaus of the Dakotas, south through New Mexico, Arizona and West Texas. Its body is reddish brown on top and buff-tinged with brown on the stomach. It measures from eight to twelve inches long with a three-inch, stubby tail.

It is said that prairie dog towns or colonies sometimes contain thousands of individuals organized into wards, with large numbers of coteries in each ward. Each coterie is headed by a male which has won his right to rule by might.

The dog's harem consists of one to four females and the young of the past two years.

The abode is a burrow, and the entrance is protected from floods by a mound of earth. In the spring, the female builds a grass-lined nest in a side tunnel of the burrow and bears a litter of five pups.

In this part of the country, the prairie dog colony appeared to be located in a flat of buffalo grass which covered a limited area and did not furnish food for a large colony. Since the animal foraged on vital grass, the stockmen influenced the Pecos County Commissioner's Court to finance the poisoning of the dogs as early as the 1920s.

The feisty little animal emits a yelp similar to the bark of a dog. Let any stranger approach, and the prairie dog sits straight as a sentinel on the mound of its burrow and barks a warning. Impending danger causes it to pop into its burrow. When shot, even if it is dead, the prairie dog almost always falls into its burrow.

Some sixty-five years ago, Judge Williams wrote:

> During the past 50 years or more, the prairie dog has multiplied in one area of Pecos County. Until about 15 years ago, we cannot attribute this increase to any direct action of white settlers. We have had sparse settlement here much earlier than this, but evidently it had no effect on the prairie dogs. With the presence of significant numbers of white settlers in this region, these marmots have experienced a decided increase in population.
>
> In 1891, I cultivated a small farm on the Pecos River, opposite the town of Grandfalls, and I drove a small town of prairie dogs off my property. Their excavations indicated that there were 20 or 25 families living in it. They moved across the fence row and set up housekeeping, from which location they have not been evicted. Several days ago I passed through this prairie dog town, and although I didn't make careful count, I estimated that there are now 200 to 300 families in the colony. This is an increase of

about 1,000 percent in 18 years. Since this prairie dog town is only about two miles from another small colony, the increase may be largely due to immigration.

There is a small, short valley just south of the Lockwood Ranch [the present Elsinore Ranch] on the road from Fort Stockton to Haymond. I have passed through it many times in the early years of my residence in Pecos County, and less frequently of late years. Either the prairie dog town in this valley now covers a larger land area than it did 25 years ago, or the population has increased significantly. The same change has taken place in the Big Canyon in the south end of this county. It was already heavily populated by these animals when I first visited it in 1885, but since then the towns have spread out over much land that was not infested with them at that time.

It can be reasonably inferred that the influx of white settlers in this county has aided the prairie dog's population explosion. The settler destroyed animals which preyed upon his flocks, and these same animals were also enemies of the prairie dog. This conclusion is not generally accepted in neighboring counties. Recently, while in the counties of Brewster and Jeff Davis, I discussed the subject with some of the oldest residents in those counties. Their lives and habits of observation prepared them to speak with some authority on the subject. Residents of Jeff Davis County were of the firm opinion that the animal had decreased in that region during the past quarter of a century. Citizens of Brewster County declared that it had neither increased nor decreased in their area.

This question is not likely to be of any practical importance. Even if the prairie dog increases during a limited settlement of the country, it will inevitably be exterminated when the country is fully settled. Farmers will quickly eradicate the little varmint for it usually occupies the land which is also best for farming. It cannot head for the hills and rocks as it cannot adapt to such an existence. Even if the country remains pastoral, it will ultimately be extirpated, though perhaps not so rapidly. Stockmen will not declare the wholesale and relentless war upon the prairie dog which will be launched by the farmers. But it does ruthlessly destroy grass, and when the cattle ranges are cut up into small pastures, the small ranchman will systematically seek its destruction. The owners of large pastures seem to consider it too irrevelant to devote much expense and trouble to its destruction.

I have often speculated upon a question related to the increase of the prairie dog. That is: How did the animal spread over the Western or Plains portion of this area in isolated colonies? From the line of the 100th meridian in Texas, and probably as far north as Nebraska, you will find the prairie dog colony system at its highest development. The area along that line is thickly populated with them. If you consider any point along that line as the original home of the animal, the gradual increase in numbers along that line is understandable. Though it has limited powers of locomotion, and is preyed upon by many enemies, you can understand how it may have spread from one home to another in the immediate neighborhood until it covered that line.

However, our prairie dog is found a great distance to the west of that line in isolated colonies. About 30 years ago I was traveling with a party on the Llano Estacado. We found a colony which we had good reason to believe was located 20 miles from any other colony. I have heard of other instances where they were much more isolated. This is where the puzzle enters the picture. The animal cannot travel far in a day, and it requires the protection of a hole to shelter it from numerous enemies. It lives on an open plain, exposed to the sight of hawks, cats and coyotes by day, and owls, coyotes and cats by night. It would appear highly improbable that a pair could successfully migrate 20 miles and found a new colony.

We know that occasionally the prairie dog partially or completely abandons a town or a part of a town. This may [be] due either to a destruction of all the grass available for food in the immediate neighborhood of its home, or it may be due to an extraordinary increase of its enemies in the immediate vicinity. Its defenses against its enemies are purely of a fugitive nature. Many people believe that it sometimes covers up a rattlesnake in its hole and abandons it for new quarters. Howell Johnson has related an incident which gives some verification to this belief. He had been told that if a rattlesnake entered a prairie dog hole, it might be driven out by quietly pouring a little loose dirt into the hole because the snake fears being buried in the hole by a prairie dog. On one occasion, he saw a snake enter a hole, sprinkled some loose dirt into it, and the snake came out. The snake undoubtedly lives upon the animal and takes possession of its home, so perhaps even if the food remains in abundance, the snakes may increase to such an extent as to cause the abandonment of the town or a portion of it.

We may assume that in an area like the Trans-Pecos country, where there are mountains and valleys, the prairie dog moved up the valleys, so that its habitations resembled lines of scattered threads lying between hills which were untenable by it. If the rattlesnakes became so numerous at one place on the thread as to cause its abandonment, then one part of the marmots moved one way and another part moved in the opposite direction, so as to leave a portion of the former line uninhabited. If the cause of the abandonment were due to the destruction of the grass then the effect could be the same. Hence, in all hill country where the line of marmot holes was hedged in and narrowed by the outlying hills, numerous isolated towns would eventually be found.

The parasitic or semi-parasitic nature of a prairie dog town has always interested me. It is not just a prairie dog colony; rattlesnakes, owls and rabbits are found in abundance around the towns. I believe you will find a rabbit there which is distinct from other breeds of rabbits. The little prairie dog owl is not found anywhere else. Hawks, crows and eagles hover around the colony, and coyotes and wild cats prowl around it. The prairie dog colony supports various animals which are divided into various classes.

The prairie dog inhabits open country which is clear of all shrubs or underbrush. The area may contain sparsely scattered mesquite trees growing from 15 to 20 feet tall, but the animal's workbench and playground must be free of dense chaparral. Evidently a bush here and there is not objectionable, but it shuns tangled thickets of underbrush. Possibly this is due to some protective instinct which guards the animal against placing its home too near effective hiding places for its enemies.

Because he insists on being in the open, Mr. Dog rarely locates his towns near water courses or ravines. In semi-arid regions, coverts of underbrush are found near waterways. Our prairie dog is found on the high open country lying between water courses. The experience of well drillers in Pecos County indicates that the animal is found where water usually cannot be reached at a depth of less than 500 feet. This habit has led to some speculation about the animal's ability to do without water, and on the location of water.

When the cattlemen moved their herds west beyond the Pecos River, water was a vital problem. Grass was abundant in Pecos County. It was not as thick as it was farther east, nor did it spring luxuriantly from the roots in a single season as it did in regions of heavy rainfall. But several years' growth of accumulated masses of grass were lying about. Much of this was still nutritious as cured hay. Water was either scant or completely lacking throughout vast areas. He who controlled the water in these regions practically owned the grass for miles around. Hence, there was great demand for watered lands, and, as a rule, such lands commanded a higher price twenty years ago than they do today.

Possession of water did not grant the owners the use of all the grass. Some of the finest varieties of grass available for grazing purposes lay in vast waterless regions beyond the reach of cattle because it was too far from surface water. Attention was directed early to the problem of securing water in these dry areas. If water could be located, large tracts of heretofore unproductive land could be turned into a source of revenue. And incidentally, the man who found the water would probably be richly rewarded for his services. The only methods of supplying water to these regions lay through building tanks to catch surface drainage from rainfall, or boring wells to an underground reservoir. For several reasons, the building of tanks was objectionable. . . .

The first practical attempts at solving the problem were made through the medium of wells. In new, unexploited country, various theories were advanced and acted upon in hopes of discovering underground water which lay at the most shallow depth. Among these theories the one most generally in vogue was that the prairie dog must have access to water, and that it attained this access through its hole. However, it was soon apparent that every prairie dog hole did not lead to water. It necessitated only a day's use of the mattock and spade to demonstrate this. Then the theory was slightly changed. It was said that there were only one or two of these holes in each town which led to water, and the other prairie dogs watered there at intervals.

Our doubting Thomas, with mattock and spade, was foiled. He could not undertake to dig up the entire town in order to discover the one fountain of water. So the altered theory long remained prevalent. I have been told that the first well in Pecos County was dug on the basis of this theory. A Mr. Ellis had it dug in 1883 or 1884, in a large prairie dog town on what was afterwards called the Slataper Ranch in Big Canyon. I think it is still in use to the present day. By some adroit management, Mr. Ellis secured the aid of Uncle Sam, and a detachment of soldiers was sent out from Fort Stockton to dig the well. With Uncle Sam backing him he succeeded in getting water, but not until he had reached a depth of about 150 feet. I think he must have been convinced that if the prairie dogs had dug down to water without Uncle Sam's help, they were indeed expert well diggers, and he must have wondered what became of all the dirt taken out of that prairie dog hole.

I have been told that other wells were drilled in this county on the basis of this theory, but they proved to be deep wells as in the case of Mr. Ellis. Although the theory lost credence, I still hear a faint echo of it now and then. It was a "wholesome doctrine and full of comfort" to the person seeking water in a country thickly populated by prairie dogs. I believe it is now understood that the prairie dog does not dig to water, but depends upon succulent grass roots when rains and dew do not furnish him with sufficient water. The wood rat, cottontail rabbit and gopher obtain the water in the same manner.

The rumor persists that prairie dogs dig to water. Who knows? Since the occupants of most prairie dog towns were poisoned in the 1930s, there is little chance to be certain. Today, most people don't care one way or another.

During the early settlement of this area, stockmen installed surface water tanks. Later, they dug wells and erected windmills with water storage tanks and water troughs. Originally, animals which required a great deal of water were confined to creeks, streams and natural ponds. Now, they can obtain water within a reasonable distance from almost any facility that stockmen use.

The lobo, raccoon, puma, lynx, bobcat, coyote and a few other animals now have a broader field in which to roam, thanks to the program of the stockmen. But most of the lobos and pumas have been exterminated along with the prairie dog. I assume there are also fewer badgers and wood rats around now than we had in the early 1900s.

The remainder of this chapter will be devoted to random observations on Trans-Pecos wildlife in general, and synopses on specific animals.

Both bald eagles and Mexican eagles take their toll on rabbits and other small animals, such as small lambs and kid goats. About 1950, I first heard that eagles were running antelope by swooping downward and making passes at them, and that the small antelope was often a victim.

Peeler Mathews, foreman of the large Elsinore Ranch, south of Fort Stockton, told me that when the eagle dived from the air and hit a running antelope on the back, it appeared that the eagle virtually lifted the back end of the animal off the ground. Quite probably, when those eagle claws stick and sink under the antelope's hide, its reflexes just naturally cause it to jump a little higher.

Charlie Stone gives us the following information on eagles: "An eagle can't see as good in the nighttime as they can in the day. So they go to roost in the night. The bobcat and panther, fox and coyote all see good at night."

Because of the recent wholesale broadcasting of sterile, male, blow flies, the deer population has shown an increase, resulting in additional profits to the stockmen. Like human beings, animals appear to be involved in a process of evolution which sometimes creates significant changes. Ranchmen in the Trans-Pecos region say that the white-tailed deer and black-tailed deer lived separately, one in the mountains and the other on the plains, and were each a distinctive breed. The deer now seem to be crossbreeding and ranchers report seeing some white-tailed deer with the long, mulelike ears of the black-tailed type. According to this, we can reasonably assume that some of the deer have changed their breeding habits.

In the pioneer days there was a year-round open season on game because the early settlers lived off of the country, Under that state of affairs the game was rapidly disappearing until laws were legislated to limit the hunting season and the game each hunter could kill.

Some forty years ago two colorful Fort Stockton residents, the late H. L. Winfield and his close friend, the late John Bennett, would take their vacations together during the hunting season and go to the U Ranch, in the Davis Mountain country located about forty miles southwest of Fort Stockton. H. L. Winfield (popularly known as Heinie), a sharp, witty man full of practical jokes, had served many years as the county clerk of Pecos County and later was a state senator for a number of years. John Bennett was a very successful businessman and rancher and had been instrumental, along with his father, in building the first telephone line to the community.

During one of their early hunting trips, Heinie maneuvered John into going out and killing a "bad bear" in the nearby chaparral. As soon as he spotted the bear, John fired and killed it. But it turned out that the animal was chained to a small tree and was the former pet of a nearby rancher. John had a hard time living that down, even if he did claim that he just went along with the frame-up although he knew it was a pet bear all the time.

Before the next hunting season, John did considerable planning for revenge. When the time arrived he made a deal with Winfield that whoever shot at and missed a deer would have his shirttail cut off by the other. The first day when coming into camp, John asked: "Heinie, wasn't that a deer you were shooting at over there?"

"No," said Winfield, "I was just practicing."

The next evening John asked again and this time Winfield told him he had shot and killed a jackrabbit. The third evening, John came up with the same question. This time, Winfield admitted that he had shot at and missed a deer. John quickly pulled out his hunting knife and whacked off a large part of the fine shirt Winfield had on. John took a look at that garment and in dismay said: "Why, Heinie, that's my shirt you've got on!"

Within the last fifteen or twenty years, the Trans-Pecos region has been invaded by the porcupine and armadillo. Neither of these animals were ever seen in this area in the early 1900s. The armadillo is a digger, and its effect on the animal and vegetable life of the region remains to be seen.

The porcupine has already begun to kill piñon trees and groves of hackberry trees. Unlike most animals, they are not in the least timid about invading towns where they will climb into the shrubs in one's yard without an invitation. I discovered one ensconced in the ligustrum just outside my kitchen.

Our neighbor's housedogs were acting up fiercely and

the neighbors assumed the dogs heard or smelled something outside the residence. They let the dogs out to catch a mean prowler — and the hapless canines charged headlong into a mean porcupine which bombarded them with sharp missiles. It required hours to remove the quills from the dogs' faces.

I turn again to Charlie Stone, who will tell us a bit about porcupines, possums, armadillos and javelinas: "I've only caught two possums and three armadillos. In this last year I've killed about seventy-five porcupines, sometimes three in one tree. They eat any kind of fruit tree and hackberry trees. They eat the inner bark.

"Some people say they've caught javelinas killing or eating sheep. I was driving along a road once and saw a javelina chasing a sheep."

The following story was related to O. W. Williams by a man named McKenna:

In 1880 the Southern Pacific Railroad was being built eastward through New Mexico. A widow with several small children was following the workers and earning a living by taking in washing for the laborers.

One evening she missed her small daughter, who was only five or six years old. A search that lasted throughout the night failed to produce the child. The following morning one of the men remembered that he had heard the burros braying and cutting up. When the men went to investigate the cause of the disturbance, they found the little girl, safe and sound with the burros. Burro tracks and lobo tracks around the site indicated that some lobos had tried to get to the child and the small burros during the night. The adult burros had formed a circle, exposing their rear ends, and had kicked the wolves until the predators gave up. Some skin and blood around the site attested to the fight those burros had made.

Predatory animals are quite frequently scroungy beasts which most of us find difficult to appreciate. Due to an increase in population in the United States, our nation is consuming more meat. In the event of possible shortages, I would prefer that animal predators be exterminated. They hamper our producers of beef and mutton, and greatly increase the risk taken by ranchers.

However, if all predators were killed, cottontail rabbits and jackrabbits would multiply rapidly and eat most of the grass upon which our livestock lives. And if we eradicated the predators which kill rattlesnakes — imagine a population explosion of these dangerous reptiles. Instead of hunting predators, we would have to organize rattlesnake hunts and rabbit drives. In addition, we would be beset with swarms of June bugs, grasshoppers, locusts and other pestilent insects which would destroy much of the fruit crop. Since we are now prevented from spraying with many insecticides, with what on earth would we ever be able to swat the hordes of insects with which we would be plagued if insect-eating predators did not help in keeping the insect population down.

Thoughtlessly upsetting nature's balance can be tricky business. It appears that we must give science time to replace the indirect services that predators perform for us.